VARIOUS

THOUGHTS

ON

POLITICS, MORALITY,

AND

LITERATURE.

By W. BURDON, A. M.

FORMERLY FELLOW OF EMANUEL COLLEGE, CAMBRIDGE.

𝕹𝖊𝖜𝖈𝖆𝖘𝖙𝖑𝖊 𝖚𝖕𝖔𝖓 𝕿𝖞𝖓𝖊:

PRINTED FOR THE AUTHOR, BY M. BROWN, IN THE
FLESH-MARKET; AND SOLD BY
WEST AND HUGHES, AND CLARKE, NEW BOND-STREET,
LONDON; AND
THE OTHER BOOKSELLERS IN TOWN AND COUNTRY.

1800.

TO THE

VIRTUOUS,

LEARNED,

AND

INTREPID

GILBERT WAKEFIELD.

THOUGHTS,

&c.

THOUGH, in my attack on the Pursuits of Literature, I had intended principally, to convey my own thoughts, on a greater variety of subjects than any other single opportunity afforded; yet my intention not being fully understood, has injured the sale of my book, and prevented that extensive circulation, which all opinions deserve relating to the peace and happiness of mankind; on this account, I have been induced to alter my design, and leave the blunders, the quotations, the egotism, the impudence, and malevolence of the Pursuits of Literature, in that oblivion to which the public seems now to have consigned that book and its anonymous author, and to make no further use of him, than as the means of conveying my sentiments on many important topics, on which we moſt completely and eſsentially differ.

THEORETICAL EXCELLENCE.

" But with this, though man might be
" happy, he will not always, or indeed long
" be ſatisfied. He will reach at perfection
" abſolute and unqualified. He forgets, that
" *theoretical perfection* in government *and*
" *practical oppreſſion* are cloſely allied." page
265. The freezing remark contained in this
ſentence, which tends to blight all the livelieſt energies of our nature, is happily contradicted by every teacher of morality, heathen and chriſtian, who are all earneſt in their admonitions to aim at the higheſt degree of moral excellence; for though there may be a point we never can arrive at, yet no poſsible progreſs can be made, without attempting ſomething which ſeems to require the full extent of our powers: the human faculties, though capable of great exertions, ſtand in need of great incentives, for man is by nature indolent. Should the reader wiſh to be farther convinced of the wiſdom and neceſsity of this continual purſuit of improvement, let him conſult the

4th

4th Essay of Dr Knox, the Dialogues of James Harris, and the last verse of the fifth chapter of St Matthew's Gospel. Political excellence can only be obtained by the improvement of individuals, as an aggregate sum must be composed of units: the best form of government in theory, can exist in practice only by the virtues of the people: the moralist and the politician have therefore a joint work to perform; the endeavours of the one are ineffectual without the aid of the other: the politician prepares the soil, the moralist sows the seed, and as there are different soils, so there are different forms of government, some of which are better adapted than others to the culture of morality; that which affords the fewest temptations to dishonesty, and leaves the greatest room for individual exertion, is the best suited to the growth of virtue, and most likely to be preserved by its own inherent excellence. Much has been said and written on the difference between theory and practice; but the dispute has hitherto been, like many others, a mere dispute about words, by mistaking the word *plausible* for *true*, and by too hasty a decision as to *true* and *false*: experience is the teſt of truth, and in all things which depend on human agents; and whatever theory or opinion is not practicable, is not true: to ſay that any thing is true in theory, and falſe in fact, is to ſay, that the ſame thing can be true and falſe, which is ridiculous: that one and one make two, is true, becauſe it is evident, and depends on nothing extraneous; that a government, purely repreſentative, is the beſt of all governments, can only be proved by experience; to maintain the contrary, is to ſubſtitute opinion for truth, and to give that weight to the ſpeculations of the mind, which is due only to the teſtimony of facts; yet on the other hand, to deny that any theory can be true, till it has received the full refutation of experience, is equally injurious to the progreſs of improvement, and the general happineſs of mankind, and both tend to reſtrain that which ought to know no reſtraint, the operation of intellect in the purſuit of happineſs. A very ſhort experience may prove ſome things to be true, while a ſucceſſion of ages is required to prove others to be falſe. Whoever denies that man is a being capable of ſocial improvement,

provement, must deny all the experience of past ages, and even of the present, yet that that improvement has its bounds, is equally certain: here seems to be the great error of many political writers, who have applied a term of unlimited extent to what in its nature must be limited, because it is possible to conceive more than it is possible to execute: had they talked of the improveability of human nature, they might have met with fewer opponents; for that the world has been progressively improved on the whole, is not to be doubted, and what has been advancing so many thousand years, it is probable is not yet compleated. The invention of man affords no surer means of promoting that improvement, than the exercise of private judgment in its utmost extent; that right has frequently been recognised, but never fully enjoyed; for even those who have pretended the most to respect it, have frequently exercised a control over public opinion, which control is, in all instances, the most dangerous tyranny to which mankind have ever submitted; because it makes them slaves without perceiving it, and seems to govern them by their own consent; and
it

it arises, like all other tyranny, from that passion which has committed greater ravages in the world, than all the rest together, the love of power: so extensive are the effects of this passion, that they are equally felt in all ranks of society, from the despot on a throne, to the despot of a private family: from setting the fashion in religion, to the fashion of a cap or a hat, and extends not only to the regulation of actions, but even of opinions; hence it is, that men have assumed the right of dictating to each other in matters not properly cognizable by human laws, and availing themselves of the power which riches, relationship, or authority, have put in their hands, have presumed to control the opinions and the conduct of others in matters which affect their own or other people's happiness, only by the importance falsely attached to them, and not by any inherent necessity in the nature of things. I feel that I am hardly able to do justice to my ideas on this important subject, and to develope, with sufficient force and clearness, the extensive miseries which have been occasioned by the assumed power of dictating to others, and the various advantages that must result from

from the exercise of private judgment. The long and bloody wars which have been undertaken in the name, and with the pretence of religion, have originated in no other motive than that of dictating to others what they ought to believe: creeds and articles of faith are derived from the same principle; and in these, as in many other instances, a few individuals have taken upon them to think for whole nations, whom their love of power led them to keep in error and ignorance. And now to go from great, to things of lesser consequence; such is the power of fashion and custom, that every singularity of manner, dress or opinions, however harmless, convenient, or rational, is stigmatized with the most opprobrious epithets, by those who are the slaves of this many-shaped tyrant. The effects of this submission, in damping the ardor of genius, and retarding the progress of improvement, is evident from the slow advances that have taken place in the world in moral and political improvement; for ages have passed, in which only a few bold spirits have dared to advance what they knew must ensure them ridicule, persecution, or odium; so that it is impossible to estimate the sum of general happiness which has been lost, by this restraint on private judgment; but these times, happily, are over, and the season is hastily approaching, when public opinion, left uncontrolled, will operate only as a restraint on vice and folly, and the exertions of genius and talents will be no longer cramped by the tyranny of fashion or prejudice: to this it need not be objected, that nothing will remain fixed or stable among mankind after such an unlimited permission to change; for such is the uniformity of truth, that nothing can be long admired, (when unsupported by authority) which is not sanctioned by the voice of sound wisdom; it is only folly which can require external support. The tyranny exercised by means of public opinion operates doubly; first, by its force on individuals, and secondly, by means of individuals on each other: some men are afraid of doing a thing, because it is not customary, others because they fear the censure of those who have no other ground for their opinions but fashion or authority, and thus act in the double capacity of tyrants and slaves. Though it may seem somewhat like a paradox, yet I will venture

venture to maintain, that all great changes of public opinion have proceeded flower in this country, confidering its freedom, than in any other, becaufe the government has been watchful to check or promote them according to its own pleafure. The Reformation, attempted by Wycliff, proceeded flowly, and was foon crufhed; and that of Luther might have fhared the fame fate, but for the capricious tyranny of Henry VIII. The Revolution of 1688 proceeded in a manner from the government; for had not the great officers of ftate joined the party againft James, his family might have been yet in power, as the prejudices of the people were in favor of his divine right. Now, in all countries where the ruling powers govern by public opinion, they are anxious to control and manage that opinion as it fuits their purpofes; where they govern in defiance of it, they are negligent of it to their own ruin: this was the cafe in France, and is now in Germany; the government think themfelves fecure by the force of the military, and defpife the opinion of the people againft them; but when that becomes fufficiently general, even the military cannot refift its power, and the government have nothing left but to yield, on the best terms they can, to a force that can be no longer restrained. Here then we stop,—and from all that has been said, I will deduce these two consequences, first, that a government may stand for a long time against public opinion, while it has the power of the sword; and secondly, that society can never receive any great improvement till public opinion ceases to be controled. To return now to our author. That theoretical excellence and practical oppression are essentially and not accidentally connected, remains yet to be proved, for the theory has never yet been fairly tried, its operation has been obstructed by events which some men attribute to the nature of things, and others to the intervention of accident: till individual reformation has been farther advanced, it is needless to expect any great political improvement; but supposing the assertion of the author, against theoretical excellence, to be true, it is no impeachment of the conduct of those who joined in applauding the first Revolution in France. Nothing had then occurred to disappoint the most sanguine expectations of the friends of liberty;

liberty; for till April, 1792, when the war began on the continent, all seemed prosperous and happy, and might have continued so, if foreign force had not interfered, but on this beaten subject I will not say any thing farther at present—time will convince those who are proof against argument.

MOTIVES TO VIRTUE.

" I have no romantick ideas of virtues
" without motives, and of actions without
" regulations. I believe it to be a matter of
" general safety, that crimes should be *dis-*
" *cerned*, as well as repressed, by legal sanc-
" tions; and that the nature of justice, and
" of injustice, should be declared, taught, and
" enforced, by law, by religion, and by edu-
" cation." p. 169. For whom this is meant, the author best knows; for though moralists have differed about the motives to virtue, yet none that I ever heard of, conceived a species of virtue without motives; but it is our author's misfortune to imagine, that all those who differ from him, must undoubtedly be fools: as to actions without regulations, he only means what he said before, it is mere words: that crimes should be discerned before

fore they can be repressed, our author is not the first man to find out, but that they should be prevented is more to be desired than either. The difference between justice and injustice is not so perplexed as to require the triple instruction of law, religion, and education, it is only by the multitude of instructors that it can become confused. Should conscience be found erroneous, to what other monitor can we trust? for conscience is only the feeling which we have of the conformity or disagreement of our actions to a standard of right.

THE CHURCH.

" By perseverance in the constitution sa-
" cred and civil *which now is.*" p. 170. Our civil constitution we are all acquainted with; it is that constitution by which our civil liberties are secured and preserved; but our sacred constitution is not quite so intelligible, for, sacred, means inviolable; and if our church is asserted to be of that nature, we are little better than papists. To call that constitution sacred, which has been acknowledged, by its best defenders, to depend, as to its form, on the will of the state, seems to be

be rather a misapplication of terms; it is bringing us back to the times of Laud and Sacheverell, which the better judgment of such men as Hoadly and Shipley had taught us to forget: they never talked of our church establishment but as the creature of the state; because they knew and confessed, that a church is but a mode of teaching christianity, and has, in different ages, varied according to the opinions of the times, from the simple επίσκοπος,* or presbyter, to the Lord Bishops of the present day; and though a protestant Bishop is rather a humbler being than a sovereign pontiff, yet both are very remote from the simple administration of the primitive times: let us then hear no more of the sacred constitution of a church, which to-day may have one form, and to-morrow take entirely another.

THE PLATONISTS.

" Thomas Taylor, translator of Plotinus,
" parts of Plato, the fable of Cupid and
" Psyche from Apuleius, Hymns, &c. the
" would-be restorer of unintelligible mysti-
" cism

---

* The words επισκοπος and πρεσβυτερος are every where used synonymously in the Epistles.

" cifm and fuperftitious pagan nonfenfe.
" All that Iamblichus revealed to Ædefius."
p. 181. Though this note ill agrees with what the author has elfewhere faid of Plotinus, vide p. 415. and in his Tranflations, p. 95. yet I fhould be forry to defend all the pagan methodifm of the latter Platonifts, or even the fublime theology of Plato; but I refpect the virtuous labors of Thomas Taylor, and I admire any fyftem of belief which leads to purity and fimplicity of manners, in an age of unprincipled profligacy. Mr Gibbon has told us of all that Iamblichus revealed to Ædefius, vol. 1. p. 65. and the Monthly Review for September, 1795, has the very words of our author, which were not publifhed till May, 1796: he beft knows from whence arifes this coincidence.

PORTRAITS.

" See in the title page to the pofthumous
" Works of Edward Gibbon, Efq. in 2 v.
" 4to. publifhed by Lord Sheffield, an en-
" graving of THE HISTORIAN OF THE
" ROMAN EMPIRE, which his lordfhip de-
" clares to be " as complete a likenefs of Mr
" Gibbon, as to perfon, face, and manner, as
" can

" can be *conceived.*"*!!!* I have no doubt of
" Lord S.'s friendship for Mr. Gibbon, but
" why hang up his friend in effigy to the
" ridicule of the present age and of all pos-
" terity?—I just remind all collectors of
" prints, that there is to be had not only the
" head of Dr. Gillies, and other historick
" cooks, of Dr. Denman the man-midwife,
" of Mr. William Coxe, traveller and friend
" to half the crowned heads in Europe,
" *with his age* at the bottom of the print,
" and of other great personages; but there
" are still left some choice proof impressions
" of the striking *head and likeness* of Mr.
" *John Farley*, PRINCIPAL COOK at the Lon-
" don Tavern, to be purchased separate from
" his great culinary work, being all that
" were left unsubscribed for by the Lord
" Mayor and Court of Aldermen, by the
" East India and Bank Directors, and by
" Mr. Pitt and the elder Brethren of the
" Trinity House." p. 185. The author's
delicacy and humanity, which seldom come
from his heart, seem here to be a little mis-
placed: if nature was not kind to Mr Gibbon in the formation of his person, why
should either he or his friends be ashamed

of

of it? Personal defects are beneath the notice of a philosopher, and he must have a pitiful spirit who can either ridicule those of others, or lament his own. Lord Sheffield certainly never could imagine that he was doing any injury to Mr Gibbon's memory, by giving a faithful representation of his person; and he has surely done a service to the world by contributing to lessen the regret at personal defects, when they see them joined to such talents as those of Mr Gibbon; littleness or deformity of person are indeed never contemptible nor pitiable, but when accompanied by similar qualities of the soul and temper. The silly sneer at the amateurs of prints only serves to shew the gentleman's own ignorance, in one branch of knowledge at least, for few people despise what they understand; or perhaps it was only meant to convey his ill-nature against Dr Gillies, whom, in spite of all his attempts to conceal it, he certainly dislikes; against Dr Denman, whose profession he makes a term of reproach; and against others, who have been honored with having their likenesses engraved, while that honor has not yet reached him. The mere desire of gathering together

together a greater number of prints than any other person, or of possessing such as are only valuable because they are rare, is certainly a very contemptible propensity, and as much deserves to be ridiculed as any other silly fondness, which has no useful design or tendency; but the desire to possess the finest specimens of one of the most elegant and ingenious arts of civilized society, or the portraits of persons in any degree eminent, is praiseworthy and useful, as it tends to promote the improvement of a pleasing art, to perpetuate the remembrance of departed excellence, and to convey an idea of the persons of those who have been distinguished from their fellow-creatures, either by their talents, virtues, or peculiarities; and if Mr John Farley possessed the art of pleasing the palates of the citizens of London better than any other cunning artificer of curious meats, I see no earthly cause why Mr John Farley should not have his portrait engraved for the pleasure of those who love good eating, as that of any other man has been engraved for their pleasure, who love to see the portraits of those who have in any line excelled; and even if our author, when he is known, had his likeness in a print, I should be happy to add it to the number I already possess of those who have in any degree acquired celebrity.

AKENSIDE.

" I will add here, that if any *young* man of
" genius, classical learning, and poetical ar-
" dour, would present the world with a
" Greek translation of AKENSIDE's " *Hymn*
" *to the Naiads*," and submit it to the correc-
" tion of an experienced Greek scholar be-
" fore publication, he might establish a learn-
" ed and honourable reputation for himself,
" and add another composition worthy of
" Homer or Callimachus." p. 191. Yet they had better let the Hymn to the Naiads alone; it is Greek already, in its mythology, its imagery, and turn of sentiment. A poem of more beautiful expression, more exquisite delicacy of feeling, and more harmonious measure does not exist in our language, the Lycidas of Milton alone excepted: yet one of these, the unfeeling Johnson has coarsely derided, and the other he has passed by in silence. To say that a translation of the Hymn to the Naiads might resemble Homer or Callimachus indifferently, is to say, that
these

these two poets are like each other: they have both written hymns to the gods, it is true, but in a very different stile; so that their resemblance is pretty much the same as Fluellen's comparison between Alexander and Harry of Monmouth, vide Henry V. In the first place, their language is different, for though the Greek language has changed less than any other in the same space of time, yet 700 years will make great alterations in any language, and this was nearly the space between these two poets. They are both admirable in their kind, yet no more like each other than an old man and a man in the vigor of youth. Homer is diffusely narrative, simple, familiar, descriptive, and sometimes tedious; Callimachus is concisely sublime, forcible, pathetic, artificial, and impressive; and whoever wishes to be convinced of this, need only read the two hymns which they have written most nearly on the same subject; that of Homer to Apollo, and those of Callimachus to Apollo and Delos; Homer sings the history of Apollo, Callimachus his praises: the one is all nature, the other all art; so much for their resemblance. Akenside is like neither of them exactly, he has more sentiment than Homer, and less sublimity than Callimachus; his compound epithets he has borrowed from the Greeks, but his are less expressive than theirs; in harmony of numbers, he is little their inferior, but in elegant and appropriate diction, he is below them, inasmuch as Greek is inferior to English: for his use of heathen mythology, he has been blamed by many tasteless lovers of propriety, who forget that the names of the heathen deities are but names for the properties of human nature, or the operations of the universe. Akenside has neither the concise sublimity of Callimachus, nor the pleasing prolixity of Homer: he sings of humbler deities than they did, and his strain is suited to his subject: as the Naiads are the sources of health, decency, and comfort, the stile in which he celebrates their praises is pure, equable, and elegant, less simple than Homer, yet more humble than Callimachus. The other works of this author are all admirable, but his Pleasures of Imagination is that on which his fame principally depends; it is one of the finest poems in our language, not merely in its poetical execution, but in its moral tendency:

dency: it is meant to exalt the finer feelings of the foul to the perception of moral pleafure, and lead them from tafte to virtue: the fublime and refined fyftem of Plato is the fource of the author's fentiments, but they are arrayed in charms which even Plato failed to give them, and had he lived to fee them fo adorned, he muft, in this inftance at leaft, have relaxed his feverity againft poets; it conveys, in every line, the moft refined and exalted ideas; it glows throughout with the love of elegance, proportion, and harmony, yet all thefe are fubfervient to the fentiments of virtue and liberty: whether his fyftem is true or not, I will not venture to decide; that it is grand and beautiful no one will deny: to me it feems that imagination has added to the charms of truth, and deduced it from an origin, at leaft doubtful, yet certainly fublime. Though this great poet was my townfman, I have frequently attempted, without fuccefs, to acquire fome information of his early hiftory; nothing more is known of him than Johnfon and Hawkins have related, and one anecdote which the diligent hiftorian of our native town has recorded, in

his

his Remarks on Popular Antiquities; that, after him, I have failed to acquire any thing new on a fubject on which he appears to have taken much pains, is not to be wondered: the truth is, our poet was little thought of in his own town, he left it early, for poetry and commerce have no connection, and after he had left it, his friends probably thought no more of him; they were low people, and could not be fuppofed able to appreciate his worth, yet he has left a name behind him which has illuftrated the place of his birth, and put to fhame his dull cotemporaries, for of all thofe who inhabited the town in his life-time, perhaps not one is now remembered,—fuch is the pre-eminence which genius can beftow.

THE UNIVERSITIES.

" This is the warning voice which fhould
" be heard, and heard *aloud* in affemblies fre-
" quent and full, in all churches and in all
" cathedrals; but chief in thofe twin-fifters
" of learning, the Univerfities of England,
" Oxford and Cambridge, which can be fup-
" ported *on thofe principles alone*, on which
" they were founded, and *by which* they have
" flourifhed."

" flourished." p. 192. As the Universities were founded on Roman Catholic principles, and have since been adapted to a protestant establishment, it is to be hoped they will still keep pace with the spirit of the times, and be ready to accede to whatever change the state, in its wisdom, may think best suited for the increase of virtue and happiness: whenever that time comes, I have no doubt its reverend teachers will yield, with that due submission which becomes christian ministers, to the will of the superior powers; no one will deny, that the defects of our two Universities, as places of education for public life, are many and great, yet notwithstanding the unrefuted remonstrances of individuals, they still remain unreformed, owing to that dread of innovation which has possessed all the privileged classes of society, and blinded them to their true interest: the evils complained of have been frequently enumerated; I will not attempt to do more than repeat them, yet every revival of the subject may make it more evident. In places where great numbers of young men, in the heat and vigor of youth, are collected together, it is almost impossible to prevent some irregularities, and

many

many follies. Yet still it behoves those who are concerned in their education, to lessen, as much as possible, the temptations to vice, to correct the effects of the more dangerous passions, and to strengthen the motives to moral and intellectual improvement; yet instead of this, a bundle of obsolete statutes supplies the place of effective regulations; the means of instruction are few, and the temptations to idleness are many and frequent: frivolous ceremonies are more regarded than moral duties, wealth and rank are more honoured than virtue and knowledge. The want of public examinations is severely felt in many colleges, for they are the only means of bringing forth what young men know, and the best inducement to add to their stores; but these examinations should be suited to all capacities, and on subjects generally useful, neither too simple, nor too difficult, and adapted to the different propensities of those for whom they are intended: for this purpose, young men ought not to be kept at a distance from their tutors; at present, these gentlemen are much too stiff and reserved; artificial dignity may suffer from too near an inspection, from too great a familiarity; but true dignity can never

never be lessened by intimacy, while it preserves a proper decorum; a similarity of pursuits, is a bond of union, with all ages and all degrees: at present, young men are left too much together; the company of their tutors, if they knew how to be familiar without losing respect, might frequently restrain them from vicious indulgences, and give support and assistance in many virtuous pursuits: at least, there are many who, I am certain, might have been so preserved from vice and indolence. Another great evil, in both our Universities, is the little attention that is paid, in most colleges, to the election of fellows, of those who are to be the future guardians of our youth: wherever this right belongs to the society, they are bound by the strictest obligation, by the will of their founder, to elect the most worthy and sufficient; yet for all this, I am sorry to say, and I say it from a painful knowledge of the fact, that this is very little attended to: for some men are elected, merely because they are good companions; others, because they show an accommodating disposition, and are not likely to disturb the affairs of the college, that is, endeavor to recall it to its original prin-

principles; others are chosen, because they are connected, by interest or relationship, with the leaders of the society; others again, because they are mere cyphers; others, because they are next in seniority, where the society wish to avoid the trouble of a contest; and others, because they are good mathematicians; but few, very few indeed, because they are men qualified by their morals, their manners, and their knowledge, to be the instructors of youth, yet this is a sacred trust, and not to be conferred lightly; in every society, therefore, where men are elected with any view to this employment, for all certainly are not, it is the indispensible duty of their electors, to consider whether their moral and intellectual endowments enable them, with zeal, affection, and steadiness, to preserve, in the most dangerous period of their lives, the unformed youth committed to their vigilance, from the snares and temptations to which they are exposed. As an ardent admirer of those institutions, which were at first founded with the noblest design, and with the most liberal munificence, I have ventured to offer a few remarks on the means of preserving them from

that

that sweeping devastation which will probably one day overtake them, if they are found wanting in the great purposes for which they were intended, for they can finally be preserved only by their own intrinsic worth.

THE ROMAN CATHOLICS.

" I allude to the grand emigration of
" French priests and others to England, at
" the late Revolution in France. (1790.)"
p. 193. To the cause of the Roman Catholics, which occupies so large a portion of the author's book, I am desirous to do justice, not from any partiality to their tenets or their discipline, but from an impartial love of justice, and compassion towards all sects and parties who are misrepresented or oppressed. The Roman Catholics, I am persuaded, are the most loyal, dutiful, and affectionate subjects in the nation, and why are they so, but from the liberal policy which has been adopted towards them in this country, so different from what they have experienced in Ireland? That there is any hope or intention, either among the clergy or the laity of that persuasion, of the restoration of their establishment, or the propagation of

their opinions, is, I believe, as deſtitute of truth, as many other chimeras of our author's invention: they know it to be impoſſible; they know that the ſtream runs the other way; and many of the moſt zealous Catholics, ſo far from looking to the reſtoration of popery, lament, with bitter tears, the general progreſs of infidelity; they know too, that as another church is endowed with the riches of the ſtate, they have little chance of making converts from that church, againſt their temporal intereſt: the author ſeems to confound popery as it is, with what it was a hundred years ago; but he is miſtaken, for the popery of the preſent day, even where it is eſtabliſhed, is not domineering nor inſulting to others; it aims at no extenſion, even of temporal power, and is limited to a very few ſtates; and, where it is not eſtabliſhed, but tolerated, it ſubmits with prudence to the will of the government: its conduct is exemplary, though its doctrines are ridiculous: it ſeeks not to diſturb others, and all it aſks is the quiet enjoyment of its own belief; yet this is the religion which the author of the Purſuits of Literature has repreſented as reſtleſs, active, and

and diffatisfied, ever feeking its own aggrandifement, and content with nothing lefs than fovereign power, and viewing, with malignity, all the eftablifhments of the earth; yet, for all this, the Quakers are not more quiet than the Roman Catholics: had they always been of this temper, the peace of the world had never been difturbed by them, nor the religion of Jefus corrupted. But fhould we allow that any danger is to be apprehended from the Catholics, it is not from their own efforts, but from the partiality of fome of our rulers to their doctrines, for, at prefent, they are by the law of the land in direct fubjection to the Church of England.——The author, p. 195, has accufed the Catholics of intolerance to men of other perfuafions; let him recollect, that the 13th article of our church exprefsly fays, that all works done by thofe who have not received the infpiration of the Holy Spirit, have the nature of fin; that is, they are not acceptable.—In p. 196, he has raifed a great alarm about a manual of the Catholics, which, from his account, I had believed to contain treafon and gunpowder plots in every line; yet this formidable engine, this fixpenny cannon,
which

which is to batter down the establishment, both in church and state; which is to dispose of the souls and bodies of all the nation, and prepare for the triumphant entry of popery into these realms, is neither more nor less, than a mere spiritual red-book for the use of Catholic communicants, and useful to them only. It contains, first, an almanack of the feasts, and fasts, and times of indulgence, with the colors of the particular vestments, to be used by the priest on each particular day, marked at the side in a capital initial letter, of different colors, which our author represents as so alarming: he could not have thought so, that is impossible, he must have meant to deceive others, by a pompous display of very simple facts; after this, follow various articles of information, useful only to Catholics, which Catholics only can desire to know, such as a list of English Papists who have suffered by a French Revolution; and a list of names of those who have taken refuge in this country, with their places of residence; an obituary of Roman Catholics; and a list of Catholic seminaries and convents: to which is added, by the bookseller, without any blunder at all, a list of of the medicines fold by him under the authority of government, like all other quack medicines. I will not attempt to expofe the gentleman's ftupid rant (for argument or evidence there is none) by any thing but facts, for they fpeak moft ftrongly of the harmlefs and inoffenfive nature of this mighty performance— The Layman's Directory; a work in which there is no inclination, no allufion, no tendency, to any thing feditious or dangerous.

DIVINITY.

A lift of books *preparatory* to the ftudy of divinity, which the author has given, and which is too long to be here inferted, might well frighten a modeft candidate for the miniftry, and make him fay with the Apoftle, "Who is fufficient for thefe things?" Now when we recollect that all thefe books, and many hundred thoufand more, were written to explain one little volume, we naturally afk, have they made it more plain or more unintelligible? In the hiftory of human learning, there is perhaps nothing more furprifing than the contraft between the fimplicity of the gofpel and the intricacy of the ftudy of divinity,

divinity. The novelties which have been introduced by men of inventive faculties, the disputes that have been raised by subtle logicians, have multiplied to such an extent, the doctrines of religion, that they serve more to perplex, than to convince, to draw men from the performance of practical duties, to the contemplation of refined subtleties, and to substitute faith for morality: belief seems now to be all that is required of a christian, nay with many, much less; to profess to be a christian is sufficient, so much has the increase of doctrines subverted the pure simplicity and honesty of christian faith: with some people, religion is a trade; with others, it is a habit, rather than a sentiment or a principle, and those who go most regularly to church, may yet be filled with vanity, malice, and avarice, with hatred and all uncharitableness: articles heaped upon articles, and ceremonies upon ceremonies, have crushed the vital spirit of christianity, and made it now no more than a name, or a bare remembrance of what once existed. Though it is not to be denied that christianity, in its present state, is very different from what it was in the primitive times, yet our church
professes

professes to hold no doctrines which may not fairly be proved out of the sacred writings; now in this they deceive themselves and others, even more than the Roman Catholics, for *they* profess to be bound by the church alone, and deny the right of private judgment in interpreting the word of God, a right on which the Protestant Church expressly rests; but in the 19th and 20th Articles, she declares, that she has *authority in matters of faith, yet that it is not allowed her to enjoin any thing contrary to God's word;* but while she claims the power of determining what is the word of God, the rest is a mere shew of humility, a mere pretence to deceive. To this corrupt state of christianity, it is not to be wondered that many still adhere, both from conviction and interest; for conviction does not always proceed from investigation, and interest attaches those who require no other proofs; to believe or profess christianity is one thing, to be a christian is another; though frequently mistaken for each other, no two things can be more different.

GODWIN.

GODWIN.

" I have given some attention to Mr. Godwin's work "ON POLITICAL JUSTICE," (first published in 2 vols. 4to; and since in 2 vols. 8vo.) as conceiving it to be the CODE of *improved* modern ethicks, morality, and legislation." p. 210. To the merits of Mr Godwin's work on Political Justice I am happy to bear my testimony of applause; it is impossible for any man to read it without having his rational faculties strengthened and improved: it holds out the strongest motives to virtue, and disguises no principle for fear of offending the prejudices of the world; such books alone do good, they go to the bottom of things, while weaker moralists rest only on the surface, and leave men just where they found them, or make them worse: it is more rational than the system of the Stoics, and more refined than that of Epicurus. The principles that were scattered in Rousseau, Hume, and Helvetius, he has gathered together into one connected system, and with some few exceptions, his book forms the most intelligible code of morality now extant. Mr Godwin's

Godwin's life and writings are those of a true and dispassionate lover of wisdom, he seeks only to instruct mankind by slow and gentle degrees, he is an enemy to all violence, either in action or disputation; he knows that men can only be improved by enlightening their judgment, and therefore he has, at all times, endeavored to repress every proceeding of an inflammatory tendency among his friends and admirers; for this he forfeited the friendship of a celebrated popular declaimer, whose intentions were at least questionable, though some people pronounced them to be evident. By those who are anxious to resist his principles, his credit is said to be on the decline, but these men forget that Mr Godwin's is not a noisy, tumultuous address to the passions of men, calculated to set the world in an uproar, but a calm, rational system, intended to develope and improve the judgment, and therefore slow in its operation, and silent in its effects: it is addressed to the individual in his closet, and not to the multitude in camps, and courts, and crowds.

JOHNSON

JOHNSON AND PARR.

"I have been misunderstood. I hold up none of Dr Parr's sesquipedalia verba to ridicule; it is his verbiage and phraseology which I reprobate. It would be ridiculous indeed to compare *the Birmingham Doctor* with Dr Samuel Johnson. I am not his Biographer It is not his life, but his writings which I criticise." page 219.— The resemblance between Dr Parr and Dr Johnson, has been perceived by many who are not very partial to either; there are the same sesquipedalian words to be found in both writers; the same pomposity of diction, the same inversion of the language: they have equally contributed to withdraw us from that simplicity which Addison and Middleton had taught us to admire, and disguised the poverty and repetition of their ideas under a heavy load of words. Johnson has taught us nothing new; he has put the common topics of instruction into a new dress, but he has made no discoveries either in science or morality: he was, therefore, not a man of genius, but of talents; for genius invents, talents only arrange, dispose,

and

and modify, adorn, compare, and compound; genius is the lot of few, talents fall to the share of many, in different proportions and degrees; some men are born to create knowledge, others to acquire it, and teach what they have learnt: Johnson had not the erudition of Parr, nor has Parr all the wisdom of Johnson; nor do we find in either of them that wisdom which lays down principles, but that which developes them; there is in both the same spirit of domineering, the same impatience of contradiction, the same blind attachment to their own belief: the one has the prejudices of a Tory, the other of a Whig; but as the latter are more liberal than the former, they are less disgusting, yet equally averse to improvement, beyond their own ideas of right; there is in both the same credulity, the same susceptibility of being flattered: the one was imposed on by the Cock-lane ghost, the other by the Shakspear manuscripts. In the powers of argument Dr Parr is certainly not inferior to his mighty predecessor, and, in strength of language, he is always his equal; yet it is to be lamented, that he has wasted his time and his talents, on subjects infinitely beneath him,
though

though he has contrived to introduce incidentally, many passages which display the full strength of his powers, on subjects which call for the fullest exertion of the most enlarged intellect, and interest the feelings of all ranks: yet even these are in danger of being lost to posterity, for few readers, in future times, will think of looking for politics or morality in a Sequel to a Printed Paper, or a Statement of Facts, &c.—This it is which sets Parr below Johnson; he has never exerted his powers directly on any subject of importance; there is only one book which will save him from being forgotten, his Tracts by Warburton; there indeed he has displayed the full extent of his powers, and exhausted the language in terms of caustic severity, in bitterness of reproof, and dignity of sentiment: yet even here we are only amused by an attack on an individual, and not improved by any developement of general principles. That Dr Parr has not written with the simplicity of Addison, is no more to be objected to him as a fault, than that an oak is not a poplar or a plane; and if excellence in writing is not restrained to one species, he deserves the praise of having exalted

that

that in which he has written to its greatest pitch. Those men who are delighted with the simplicity of Addison, it will certainly not please; but those who admire something more animating, and more impressive, it will not fail to delight. Dr Parr's singularity consists more in the arrangement than the choice of his words; he has not always the pompous terms of Johnson, but who will deny that he often imitates him? there is in both the same dilation of ideas, the same verbosity, the same inversion of the language in forced and awkward sentences; there are, however, on the whole, more points in which they resemble each other than in which they differ. Our author has only compared the nature of their works, not their merits as writers. " What has Dr Parr written?" is a fair question; but we ought also to ask, how he has written. " A sermon or two, rather long;" does this detract from the merits of a sermon, or say of it all it deserves? " A Latin Preface to Bellendenus, (rather
" long too) containing a cento of Latin and
" Greek expressions applied to political sub-
" jects:" is this a just character of the happy ingenuity with which classical quotations are

applied

applied to modern events? with which learning, the most minute and extensive, is rendered subservient to politics, and ancient writers describe living characters: it is a work of unrivalled learning, memory, and brilliancy. " Another preface to some Eng-
" lish tracts:" this is no character of that preface, which is certainly the finest philippic in the language. " And two or three
" pamphlets about his own private quar-
" rels:" if any of his readers can suffer their judgment to be misled by such empty assertions, they must be more inclined than they ought to be to take opinions upon trust; a more unfair attempt was never made to bias the public against a great man; for without saying a word of the merits of his writings, he has endeavoured to make it believed, that they are worthy of little notice or regard. In the enumeration of Dr Parr's works, the author has, with his usual want of candor, omitted to mention that which does him most credit, by its language, spirit, and sentiments; I mean the Letter to the Dissenters of Birmingham, from a Citizen of Irenopolis, which, though it does not bear his name,

has

has never been difowned by the Doctor or his friends.

"Dr Parr publifhed at Birmingham what
"he called "*A printed paper;*" and after
"that, "A Sequel to a *printed Paper*," a very
"large pamphlet, *de omni fcibili*, as ufual."
p. 221. This is a proof that our author has either intentionally mifreprefented Dr Parr, or never read his works, for it was not the Doctor who publifhed a printed paper, but as the title expreffes, a Sequel to a printed Paper, written by another perfon: it is even ridiculous to fuppofe, that he wrote both the Paper and the Sequel, to which it is an anfwer; as to all that wafte of learning which the gentleman has employed to ridicule Dr Parr, or perhaps to gratify his own vanity, it is ufelefs to either purpofe; it is trifling and ridiculous, and has neither humor nor vivacity.

MR HAYLEY's LIFE OF MILTON.

"Mr Hayley wrote a long life, or rather
"a fort of defence of Milton, as I think, pre-
"fixed to Boydell's grand edition of the
"poet. I like neither the fpirit nor the exe-
"cution of Mr H.'s work." p. 223. Our

author finds fault with the spirit and the execution of Mr Hayley's work, yet nothing can be more amiable than the one, though the other is not faultless. The life of Milton was written with the purest intentions, to vindicate the character, not the principles of the great poet, from the unjust asperity of his merciless biographer; the stile is sometimes redundant, and not always correct, yet these are trifles compared to the mild and candid sentiments of its amiable author: it is evident he is no friend to the republican principles of Milton, yet his love of justice and impartiality will not suffer him to believe, from an accurate examination of his life, that he was not actuated by the purest motives; and he every where cautiously distinguishes between his intentions and principles; he sees no ground to impeach the one, though he cannot approve the other: how different is this from the gross, indiscriminating violence of Johnson, who uses every occasion to vilify the poet's character, to exaggerate his failings, and conceal his virtues; for he seemed to believe, that no man can be a republican upon principle, yet nothing can be more illiberal than to impeach a man's honesty

nesty for mere difference of sentiment, for when his actions neither tend to power nor emolument, it is right to suppose that the love of justice is his only motive; this was the case with Milton, he neither sought for nor obtained riches, his only object was to instruct mankind, and he was as far exalted above the common pursuits of interest or ambition, as the fame he has acquired is above the common lot of mortality; his life was untainted by a single act of vice or meanness, and his soul, which was pure from the hands of his Maker, returned to him unsullied by the world: his language was congenial to his feelings, and displays a happy union of energy and sweetness, a peculiar turn of expression, which has never yet been equalled, and will probably never be excelled: it was meant simply to express, not to adorn his thoughts, and if it is superior to that of others, it arises only from the superiority of his ideas: in his poetry there is a spirit approaching to divine, and in his prose a force and energy never to be equalled; when these cease to be studied and admired, it may safely be pronounced, that taste, liberty, and virtue are on the decline. To return now to Mr Hayley,

Hayley, who has given the author of the Purfuits of Literature fo much offence, though what it is that has offended him he has not chofen particularly to exprefs: I fear it is the fpirit of truth, candor, and juftice, which are every where apparent in that beautiful work; if fo, I leave him to the chaftifement which every man muft feel who is poffeffed by oppofite fentiments; but I will do him the juftice to fay, I do not believe he has ever read that moft pleafing piece of biography, in our language; for if he had, and is not the moft hardened bigot that ever exifted, he could not condemn a work fo amufing and fo honorable to its author's feelings: he has heard, moft likely, that it was written to juftify Milton againft the mifreprefentations of Johnfon, and therefore took it for certain that it contained an approbation of all his republican conduct and principles.

COUNT RUMFORD.

" See the Experimental Effays, Political, " Economical, and Philofophical, by BEN-" JAMIN Count of RUMFORD, &c. &c. &c." p. 224. Though Count Rumford certainly deferves credit for his cheap inventions, and

they

they might have been of great service in Bavaria, where the poor were literally left to starve for want of employment, yet I am sorry that the poor of this country should ever be dependent upon soup shops and digesters for their support; wherever they cannot maintain themselves by their industry, in a country like this, which boasts of monopolizing the trade of the world, there must be something wrong in the distribution and circulation of its wealth, for the poor have a right to be fed plenteously, as well as the rich. I am not desirous to confound the distinction of ranks, by pulling down the opulent and wealthy, yet I am for raising the poor to a condition of ease and comfort, not independent of their industry, but the consequence of it; for I hesitate not to maintain, that when a man, in any country, cannot support his family by the sweat of his brow, he has a right to say, that he is treated unjustly: the poor are the strength and sinews of the state; it is a matter of prudence then, as well as of justice, to provide that they enjoy health, plenty, and independence; without this, their superiors may

suffer

suffer as well as themselves: it is mistaken policy to deny any set of men their rights.

THE BISHOP OF LANDAFF AND MR GIBBON.

" I would also particularly recommend the "perusal of the Sixth Letter of the Series of "Letters which the Bishop addressed to Mr. "Gibbon." p. 224. Notwithstanding our author's assertion, I am of opinion, that a more flimsy, superficial apology for christianity never was written To an affectation of candor and liberality it is alone indebted for its success; and yet for this true christians did not thank him, and unbelievers smiled at his weakness. This is, perhaps, not the time to point out particularly where the Bishop has failed to remove the objections of the infidel, yet it is by no means difficult. Though there are perhaps no two characters more different than those of Bishop Watson and Mr Gibbon, yet there is no doubt the objects of their public life were the same, and these were, fame and preferment: the one sought to obtain the great object of his pursuit by an appearance of plainness, bluntness, and sincerity; the other feared to offend the
pre-

prejudices of the world, by an open, manly declaration of his sentiments, and therefore dealt out his malevolence in dark and disingenuous sneers, and courted the favor of the great by the mean artifices of insinuation and flattery: the reward of the one was disappointment and disgust, the other is not yet in a state to receive the final decree of the public, on his life, character, and services.

MR ROSCOE.

" The Life of Lorenzo de Medici, called " the Magnificent, by William Roscoe," 2 vol. 4to. p. 228. Though I admire the classical elegance and liberal spirit of Mr Roscoe's work, I will not consent to bestow upon it all the praise of our author; for though he has done all he has done, well, yet he has omitted many things which are required in a work of that nature: he has not gone to any great depth on any subject, but particularly on the revival of literature, and the origin of the Italian language; they are subjects that require a greater depth of research than I have it in my power to undertake at present. Mr Gibbon has partially glanced at the first, in his last volume, for
his

his history ends where that subject begins; yet it is to be lamented that he bestowed so much time on the dark ages, and has left in darkness the history of the revival of learning, to illustrate which his talents and erudition were so admirably adapted. The other subject has been slightly noticed by Dr Burney, in his second volume of the History of Music; but, as he has adopted an opinion contrary to that of the learned, accurate, and industrious Giannone, I am inclined to believe he is mistaken, though, from the authority of Muratori, Maffei, and Crescembini, he has asserted that the Italian language had not acquired any consistency before the end of the twelfth century; for though I have not these confused and ponderous authors at hand to consult, yet I have the luminous page of Giannone before me, and he expressly says, it had taken root and vigor towards the end of the ninth century. —Hist. di Napoli. lib. 4. cap. 10. sec. 2. The Bulgarians, about the year 668, were introduced into the country of Naples; and though they had not forgot the use of their own language, in the year 830, yet they also spoke Latin, says P. Warnefrid, who lived

in

in the ninth century. "By which," says Giannone, "we are not to understand that "they spoke the Roman Latin, which, at "that time, was fallen into disuse, and only "retained in writing, and even there much "corrupted; and a new, popular, and com- "mon language, which had arisen from "the mixture of many strange languages, "was now intoduced into Italy, and called "Italian. So early as the time of Justinian, "Fornerius speaks of a public instrument at "Ravenna composed in that language, which "is called the vulgar tongue of Italy, and "Constantine Porphyrogenitus calls Bene- "vento and Venice, Citta Nova in Italian in "the year 910." Now these are proofs, and he has given many others, that the Italian had acquired great stability in the eleventh century; but by what means it arrived from rude corruption to vigor and elegance, it is now almost impossible to discover. The present orthography of the Italians may lead us, in some instances, to find out the pronunciation of the Latin, and to see how it became corrupted: for I have no doubt that one of these corruptions arose from the vulgar mode of the common people in writing as they speak; for instance, the word *oggie*, in Italian, is evidently a corrupt mode of spelling *hodie*, in Latin, for the meaning is the same in both, and it is also a proof that the Romans pronounced *hodie* as if it was written with two *g's*.—*giorno*, in Italian, is also corrupted from *hodierno*—*latte* from *lacte*; for it is to be remarked that the ablative case of the Latin generally forms the nominative of the Italian. *Bocca*, was probably the pronunciation of *bucca*; *fede* is from the ablative of *fides*, which was therefore most likely pronounced *fedes*; *ostro*, the ablative of *auster*, spoken also most probably *oster*; *otto* from *octo*, which was pronounced *otto*, to avoid the harsh sound of the two consonants *ct*. I might go on with a hundred other instances, but these, I trust, will suffice to convince my readers, that the pronunciation of the Italians was derived from that of the Romans, wherever the orthography of the one seems to have been taken from the pronunciation of the other. This, I should trust, will lead others to further researches on this subject, who have better means than I have to ensure them success; for many books are required, which are not to be met with

with in a distant province, remote from the center of information and literature.

A NEW TRANSLATION OF THE BIBLE.

" I mean the Preface to the *Second* volume of Dr. Geddes's *Transl<.>tion of* the Bible. I really would not trust myself to criticise the Translation itself, after I had read the fifth Chapter of Judges, v. 30. where for the words, " To every man a damsel or two," Dr. Geddes *translates* by way of a *spirited* and *inviting* improvement, " A Girl, a couple of girls, *to each* brave man." p. 243. To those who are desirous of seeing the Bible in a good English dress, it must be matter of regret, that no such thing has yet appeared; not one attempt of the kind has been conducted with propriety and decorum, all have studied to depart, as far as possible, from the old version, while they ought to have done exactly the reverse; for all that is required, is to remove a few indecencies, a few inaccuracies, and a few difficulties, arising from the change which has taken place in our language, since the time it was translated; it is now become like an old picture, which needs only to be touched up and revived, without being altered, for there is a simplicity in the old language, now sanctioned by long use, which cannot be improved on the whole, though it may be amended in particular passages.

DR HUSSEY.

" Hear Dr. Hussey the titular Bishop of Waterford in Ireland in his late pastoral Letter. "THE CATHOLIC FAITH (i. e. the tenets, the doctrines, the superstitions, the absurdities, the follies, the cruelty, and the tyranny, of the Church of Rome, and whatever makes it to differ from any other *external* establishment of Christianity) *The Catholic faith* (says his *titular* Lordship) is suitable to *all* climes, and *all* forms of government, monarchies or *republicks*, aristocracies or DEMOCRACIES." (p. 9.)" p. 262. By great good fortune I was indulged with a sight of this Pastoral Letter, and was happy to find it totally different from what it is represented by the author of the Pursuits of Literature, as might be easily supposed; for whoever knows any thing relating to the state of Ireland, during the late rebellion, must muft know, that the fuperior ranks of the Catholic clergy exerted their utmoft endeavors to prevent their different flocks from joining the forces of the rebels; and of this fact government are well convinced. Dr Huffey is one of thofe liberal and amiable men who do honor to any caufe or country, and his Paftoral Letter is written in that fpirit of mild benevolence which particularly diftinguifhes the Catholics of the prefent day from their predeceffors in more diftant times. The Bifhop's ideas of a man of true liberality are fhamefully mangled and mutilated by the illiberal critic; and I am forry it is not in my power to give them at length; they are the moft liberal that could come from a man who has any religious belief of his own, and yet refpects that of others; his advice to his clergy, on the fubject of education, is no other than might have been given by a Proteftant Bifhop on the fame fubject, nor different from what Chrift gave to his Apoftles, Matt. xviii. ver. 15, 16, 17; no proteftant could fee with indifference his children brought up in the faith of popery, and why fhould not a papift be equally zealous? not furely becaufe the one is only tolerated, and the

the other established. Dr Huffey's advice to the Legiflature, on the fubject of Catholic emancipation, is dictated by found wifdom, and a knowledge of the ftate of the world; pains and penalties now only ferve to exafperate. The Bifhop's advice throughout deferves to be contrafted with the compulfory means which he fpeaks of being ufed to bring the Catholic military to the churches of the Proteftants; his character of the Roman Catholic church, as being fuited to all forms of government, only means, that, like chriftianity, it interferes with none; it is to be wifhed it had always been fo. The allufion, in the note, to the attention Dr Huffey has received from the government of Ireland, relates to a miffion with which he was entrufted abroad, and to his appointment to a prefidency of a papift feminary in his own country.

FRANCE.

" When I confider the *future* condition of
" Europe under the revolutionary tyranny
" of France, in principles, morals, and go-
" vernment I mufe upon the awful ftrain of
" the Florentine poet:

" Si

" Si trapassammo per sozza mistura
" Dell 'ombre e della pioggia, a passi lenti,
" Toccando unpoco *la vita futura!*"

Page 251. The above was written at a time when France suffered under the severest tyranny any nation ever experienced, a tyranny which grew up in a state of war, and furnished a pretext for its continuance; but now, since one great man has changed the face of things, the same pretence no longer exists: he has fought for peace when France was humbled, and when she was victorious; and if hereafter he should be successful in overturning the machinations of his enemies, let us hear no more of his ambition, his tyranny, or his cruelty. Should the calamities of intestine war ever visit this country, and they seem every day to be coming nearer to us, let no negative or active supporter of the ministry, who suffers in his person, property, or comfort, wonder or repine at the just retribution which falls heavily upon him; for that which he has contributed to inflict on others he justly deserves to feel. To suppose that a peace can be preserved, or even signed, between the republic of France and the powers with which she is at war, betrays a gross
igno-

ignorance of human nature, which, one should have thought, ten years of dear-bought experience might have corrected. The strength of the French republic, wielded by such a man as Bonaparte, is enough to overturn all that oppose him. What he has done, ought to convince us what he can yet do, when his powers are fully exerted.

AUTHORS.

" I would declare also to *them*, that I de-
" livered it as A LITERARY MANIFESTO
" *to this kingdom* in a season unpropitious to
" learning or to poetry, in a day of darkness
" and of thick gloominess, and in an hour
" of turbulence, of terror, and of uncer-
" tainty." p. 275. To his poetry or his learning the author of the Pursuits of Literature has no right to say, that the season is unpropitious, the public have called for them again and again, and pronounced the *decies repetita* of Horace: yet are they deserving this reiterated applause, this accumulation of kindness; I have, and I trust not vainly, attempted to shew that they are not, and that the public have been deceived: the author has written in times favorable to all
the

the advocates of established authority;* for however feeble their arguments, or however flimsy their stile, they find a ready reception with all those who are prepared to resist innovation in every shape, and to embrace with eagerness every new succor against the progress of their fears: such men do not deeply weigh the merits of those who are on their side, they are not nice in the praise of their defenders; to be with them is sufficient merit, to be against them is sufficient blame; to this cause it is to be attributed, that the author of the Pursuits of Literature has found so many admirers, who give him credit for his learning, because they wish him to be learned, and praise his poetry, because they wish to believe him a poet; such are all those whom fear has made his friends; he, therefore, of all men, has the least right to say that the times are unpropitious to learning and to poetry: others, indeed, may with

greater

---

* As a proof of this, I might instance many political pamphlets, which have been much read and admired, but one is sufficient, the Considerations on the State of Public Affairs, supposed to have been written by a noble Lord, but in truth by a hireling writer of the Treasury, who seems to have inherited the tyrannical sentiments of his great progenitor.

greater justice complain, yet is the age, on the whole, not regardless of genius or talents; for if we read Ralph's Cafe of Authors, and Pierius de Infelicitate Literatorum, it will be found, that our times are less to be reproached than others with the neglect of learning and talents. A remarkable instance of private patronage has lately happened in the protection an amiable poet in humble life has received from the learned, industrious, and spirited Capel Lofft, who has introduced into the world, with splendid decorations, and an ill-written preface, * a poem, which gives the hope and promise of something more correctly elegant.

ANCIENT POETRY.

" Two lines from Sir Walter Raleigh's " Sonnet, prefixed to Spenser's Fairy Queen." p. 284. The difference between antient and modern English poetry is generally acknowledged, even by those who are ignorant wherein it consists, but to which the superiority on the whole belongs, is not so easily decided, nor where the distinction begins.— As to the first point, in my opinion, the difference

* Bloomfield's Seasons.

ference confifts both in the language, and the fentiments; in the former, without doubt, modern poetry is more polifhed and refined, yet it has loft much of the antient fimplicity, which fome modern poets have attempted to revive, by the ufe of old words; in this refpect, it muft be acknowledged, that the fuperiority belongs to the moderns, as they fometimes unite antient fimplicity with modern elegance; and, on the fecond point, though many beautiful ideas are to be found in antient poetry, yet they are frequently buried under fuch a load of quaint, conceited, forced, unnatural, and frigid thoughts, that, in many poets, their beauties hardly reward the length of the fearch. In fertility of invention, and richnefs of imagination, the moderns are certainly excelled by the antients, yet this luxuriance frequently requires the pruning hook of judgment, which it is furprifing their acquaintance with the claffics had not fuggefted, and for want of which, many of their beauties are loft in their deformities. It has lately been the fafhion to felect thefe beauties, and to publifh them unincumbered with the trafh that furrounds them, and this has, in many inftances, been done with great judgment: it is difficult to find any piece of poetry more antient than Milton, which is not disfigured by some quaint thoughts or aukward expressions; whereas in modern poetry, of the first rank, many pieces are to be found unalloyed with a single barbarism, such as in the poetry of Pope, Parnell, Gray, Dyer, and Akenside; and even those who do not arrive to the highest degree of excellence are free from the faults of the ancients, prolixity, quaintness, dryness, awkwardness, and insipidity: yet I see, with regret, the return of some of these faults in the tedious, unnatural effusions of some modern poets, who, in their great anxiety to be publishing, ransack their port folios for all they can find, and, like the antients, regard quality less than quantity; for the two volumes of the English Anthology might, without any loss to the public or the reputation of its authors, be reduced to one: it can hardly be supposed, that many of our antient poets ever corrected their works, as they contain such evident marks of haste and negligence. Now with regard to the distinction of ancient and modern poets, I think Milton and his cotemporaries are between the two, for they are strictly neither;

neither; his language partakes somewhat of the antient, yet is more polished than the times of Mary and Elizabeth; and his ideas are chastened with all the purity of classical taste and elegance; what he and his successors wanted in refinement, was completed by Pope; after him our poetry may have degenerated, but in this respect it cannot improve. In the long series of five hundred years, from the first rude attempts at poetry to the present times, many and various are the ideas that have been emitted, and much space do they occupy; but were the essence, the spirit, the finer particles of them refined and separated from the grosser feculence, the substance of them might be much reduced. Pope is one of the few among the modern poets who has no need of this chemical process; among the ancients there is not one; herein consists the difference. The verses of Sir W. Raleigh, which the author has quoted, are to be found among the many quaint congratulations to the author of the Fairy Queen, and have nothing to recommend them but a sweetness of expression which is peculiar to the ancient writers, and which is one of Sir Walter's greatest claims to the name of poet: his Silent Lover

has

has delicacy and feeling, and his Soul's Errand, though somewhat quaint, has truth and force; his other little verses abound with the faults of the age, low, forced, and unnatural thoughts, and deserve very little praise. The Sonnet is a species of poetry first invented by the Italians, and adopted only by the writers of our own country; the French have no such thing, for as it is employed solely on serious subjects, the natural gaiety of that nation is not suited to any thing so monotonous and plaintive. Among English writers the sonnet had long been disused, till Mr Edwards, the author of the Canons of Criticism, published his, about forty years ago, which are very flat and prosaic; and since him, there have been numbers. The length of this poem, every one knows, is limited to fourteen lines, divided into two unequal parts of eight and six; in the legitimate sonnet, the first, fourth, fifth, and eighth lines rhime to each other; in the last six, the rhimes are alternate. A writer, in the New London Review,* has fancifully divided the sonnet into five different sorts, the simple, the picturesque, the embellished, the pathetic, and the sublime; but these different characters

* VOL. 2d.

ters are never found so distinctly in any one sonnet, as to entitle it solely to that name. Upon the same principle he might have added another, as satire sometimes prevails, particularly in those of Milton; but the fact is, that these different qualities are only to be found mixed and combined in different sonnets. The original design of this poem was to express the feelings of love; but it soon departed from its first purpose, and is now become the vehicle for any serious and plaintive feeling. Milton, whose caustic humor prevailed in most of his writings, often used it for purposes of satire. The sonnet requires a precision, both of words and ideas, not very easy to be attained by men of lively imaginations; a unity and simplicity of thought, not requisite for any other species of poetry; and a delicacy of feeling, which few men are so happy as to possess; so that, upon the whole, though the sonnet is apparently an easy and trifling sort of poetry, it requires a union of the rarest and choicest poetical talents; hence it is, that so few have excelled in this species of writing, and that those who have excelled, have either written no other sort of poetry, or written it in a

stile

ſtile very inferior to their ſonnets. The Earl of Surrey was one of our firſt ſonnet writers; Sir W. Raleigh has alſo written one or two; but neither thoſe, nor his other poems, riſe above mediocrity. Spenſer alſo wrote ſome, but, except for the meaſure, they are little ſuperior to proſe; and they are debaſed too by the forced, unnatural thoughts of the times. A collection of theſe, among other poems, paſs under the name of Shakſpeare; but I doubt whether they were written by him. Daniel is the next in rank as to time, but ſuperior in point of beauty to the former. Drayton too has ſonnets, which he calls Ideas, ſome of which are beautiful, yet moſt of them abound with awkward and unnatural conceits. Drummond is among the old poets, the moſt beautiful writer in this ſort of poetry, yet not without the low conceits of his cotemporaries. As Milton is perhaps the beſt writer of ſonnets till modern times, his may demand a more particular criticiſm. Few of them are debaſed by any frigid conceits, and they all poſſeſs that unity of thought which is the firſt requiſite of a ſonnet, yet the lines are ſometimes harſh, and the language coarſe and familiar, though

it

it is generally precife, expreffive, and harmonious. The firft ends awkwardly with the words 'am I.' The firft line of the eighth is harfh, familiar, and abrupt—

> Captain, or colonel, or knight in arms.

The eleventh is wholly ludicrous. The fame may be faid of the 13th line of the 14th fonnet—

> Up they flew fo dreft.

In the 23d is a very harfh line—

> Purification in the old law did fave.

> Love, fweetnefs, goodnefs, in her perfon fhined,—

Is a harmonious line, but not exactly correct, for *fhined* fhould be *fhone*. The fonnets of our other ancient poets are too numerous to be criticifed minutely; but I will give fpecimens of the beft, among the Additions, as they are not every where to be found, and well deferve to be reprinted.——To fpeak in terms of juft admiration of the rich, boundlefs, varied, brilliant, and inexhauftible imagination of Spenfer, is hardly poffible; nothing in our language, nor in any language, in that point, equals him; yet the length of his Fairy Queen, the frequent repetition of language and ideas, and the unavoidable dullnefs of allegory, which even his imagination cannot every where enliven, render this wonderful poem tedious and fatiguing; but there is a charm in his language and ideas which every man of poetical taste must feel and acknowledge: he has been blamed for his affected use of old words, yet these have considerably added to the beauty of his language, and given it an air of plaintive simplicity, which is not to be found in the more polished diction of his successors, or even of his imitators in modern times.—— Spenser is a poet who seems to have been less conversant with life than any other before or after him; he has created a world of his own, in which human characters are little concerned; of the passions in general he seems to have had some idea, but in quick and accurate conception of their different effects, he is infinitely deficient, which makes his poetry so little interesting to common readers; for whatever soars much above common life and manners, cannot long be admired. No man can read Spenser for a while without being charmed, nor for long, without being fatigued; his invention is copious, but misapplied; he was led into tedious and crude conceits by the perverse

taste

taſte of the times; he was for ever ſeeking after forced analogies, and delighted with myſtical numbers and allegorical devices; for he tells Sir W. Raleigh, in his letter of introduction, that he meant to pourtray in prince Arthur, before he was king, the twelve moral private virtues, as Ariſtotle had deviſed; and if he found them well received, to frame the other twelve books on the politic virtues, in his perſon, after he was king; ſo much for the lawleſs invention of an antient Engliſh poet: he goes on and ſays, that in the twelfth book, the Fairy Queen was to keep her feaſt for twelve days, on which twelve ſeveral adventures happened, which being undertaken by twelve ſeveral knights, were in twelve books to be ſeverally handled: for the world's ſake and his own, God be thanked, he lived but to finiſh ſix of theſe quaint devices; yet, though we lament the awkwardneſs of his invention, we muſt admire the richneſs of his imagination, which was able to fill up and adorn with ſuch ſplendid images, the dry and tedious harſhneſs of continued allegory. Whether Spenſer had borrowed any of his ideas, in his allegorical perſonages, from former writers, it is now not easy to determine, yet there is one from whom he might have received a useful lesson in the government of his invention and fancy. The original designer of the Mirror for Magistrates, Sackville Lord Buckhurst, was a poet who, in clearness of conception, and strength of language, was not excelled by any of his predecessors, and his Introduction to the History of the Duke of Buckingham has immortalised him with all true admirers of poetry. I will not injure his ideas by partial quotation, but, as his poem is now extremely rare, I will give the choicest parts of it at the end of this work, among the Additions. The author of this wonderful piece of poetry was a minister of state in the reign of Queen Elizabeth, but in that department little is known of him, for politics have no alliance with poetry, they are seldom seen in the company of each other—*non bene conveniunt nec in una sede morantur*, Juv.—He was the author also of a tragedy called Gorboduc, the first dramatic piece, says H. Walpole, of any consideration in our language; as I have never seen it, I will not venture to pronounce. Certainly it is somewhat remarkable, that two of our

first

first antient poets had each an immediate predecessor, from whom, if they did not, they might have borrowed many ideas: Chaucer was immediately preceded by the author of Pierce Plowman's Vision, who, in strength of conception and coloring, was not his inferior, and Spenser, as I have already remarked, immediately succeeded Buckhurst, to whom he was not equal in judgment and correctness, for the pictures of the former are never over-charged nor crowded. It is somewhat singular, that in a work, entitled the Lives of the English Poets, that of Spenser is not to be found; and still more so, that in another book, professing to treat of Belles Lettres or Polite Literature, under the department of poetry, the name of this celebrated poet is not even named, except for his versification; now this can only be accounted for by supposing that the author has copied his remarks from those who had never mentioned him, and being unacquainted with him, as well as with all our other antient poets, he could give no opinion of his own; but this is an instance of unpardonable ignorance in a man

who

who undertakes to direct the public taste and studies.

JACOB BRYANT.

" Jacob Bryant, Esq. Author of the Ana-
" lysis of Ancient Mythology, &c. &c &c.
" See his character in the Second Dialogue
" of the P. of L. to which I refer." p. 292.
Hardly is it possible to produce an instance of deep and extensive learning worse applied than that of Mr Bryant: it has been wasted in defending paradoxes, which were no sooner raised than overturned, and are not in themselves amusing, nor supported by the powers of fancy, by vigor of stile, nor strength of argument; no man has more learning nor less judgment, nor done more harm to the cause he wishes to defend: like the elephants mentioned by Livy, he overturns the ranks of his friends instead of his enemies. His remarks on the divine mission of Moses, in his account of the plagues of Egypt, from p. 211 to 227, afford a striking illustration to all that Mr Volney has said on the origin of religion in the antient world. His doubts on the existence of Troy go to shake the credibility of all historical and tra-
ditional

ditional evidence, and his Remarks on Chriſtianity is the drieſt book on the ſubject, by many degrees: his virtues and his age are venerable, but after his death, his works will not long be remembered.

GOTHIC ROMANCE.

" I mean by theſe and ſeveral following
" lines to obſerve, that the *Pagan* Fable is
" now exhauſted, and the ſpecious miracles
" of *Gothic* Romance have never of late
" years produced a poet. Perhaps the latter
" were more adapted to true poetry than the
" pagan inventions." p. 294 All mythology is adapted to poetry, becauſe all mythology is fiction; yet though that of paganiſm may be exhauſted, it does not follow that the miracles of Gothic Romance are calculated to produce more ſublime effuſions of the Muſe; that depends on the genius of the poet, not on the nature of his materials, for theſe he can mould to his purpoſe. The tales of Gothic enchantment, their caſtles, dwarfs, and giants, may be amuſing to children, as being marvellous and incredible, but they cannot arreſt the attention of men, like the hiſtories of Jupiter, Mars, or Venus, to whom

whom are attributed human actions and human paſſions, and who are objects of worſhip rather than of terror. The gods of the Goths, like their worſhippers, are fierce and cruel; their heaven is the ſeat of ſavage enjoyment; and their hell is chilled by perpetual froſt: ſuch are the effects produced on the imagination by the difference of climate. The diſtinction between Celtic and Gothic ſuperſtition has never been ſufficiently attended to; from the Celts we have derived the tales of the Bards and Druids, which form the ſubject of Welch poetry, and the ſublime lyric poem of Gray, the fineſt our language has produced; from the Goths we derive the tales of Odin, and the fictions of the Edda, the witches and enchantments of the middle ages, and, in later times, the romantic ideas of chivalry. The Celtic ſuperſtitions remain now in Ireland, Wales, and Scotland alone, for in theſe nations only are to be found any remains of the Celts; Mr Pinkerton has placed this ſubject in its true light. The ſpecious miracles of Gothic Romance have produced ſome poets, but thoſe of no great eminence. Jerningham is, as uſual, flat and inſipid; Hole is ſometimes

vigo-

vigorous, but too frequently digressive; Sayers has many brilliant passages of genuine and sublime poetry, but he is sometimes tedious.

PUBLIC SEMINARIES.

" Eton School, like many other great
" and useful publick Schools, stands in need
" of many *new* and *strong* regulations, which
" the interests of this kingdom, in common
" with the demands of the time, call for with
" a voice not to be disregarded by the mas-
" ters and governors." p. 305. The whole note, which is too long to be inserted, relates to the reform of many gross corruptions in the conduct of our great seminaries, and of Eton in particular, which is perhaps more extensively corrupted than any other: to almost all that our author has said on this subject, I give my hearty consent; but I will tell him, that while education is considered as a trade, and till other great reforms are compleated, that school will never be otherwise than it is at present, for there is a mass and accumulation of interest extending through every department of the institution, which can never be dissolved or counteracted till the

whole is new modelled; and it will then become the legislature to consider, whether the great ends of education, viz. public and individual improvement, are best answered in large seminaries, or under the eye of parental vigilance. Education is not merely the acquisition of learning, but the formation of the heart and temper; and were parents qualified and disposed to attend to those minutiæ, which, from their earliest infancy, affect the future dispositions of their children, much of the corruption and depravity of the world might be prevented: if then the fault is in the parents, as our author justly remarks, how is that fault to be amended? "*A good tree cannot bring forth evil fruit, neither can a corrupt tree bring forth good fruit,*" Matt. vii. 18. A state, corrupted by luxury and riches, cannot bring forth men of pure morals and integrity; it is foolish to expect impossibilities. Rome afforded but a few solitary instances of virtue after she had engrossed the riches of the world. Though many objections have been urged against the present mode of classical education, yet I by no means agree to them all; for I should no more consent to read the classics in translations than to

drink

drink a mineral water a hundred miles from the Spa; the spirit of both must evaporate: but though I allow that the present mode of teaching Greek and Latin is faulty, and that much of the time consumed on it is wasted, yet it by no means follows that the custom should be omitted entirely. The first fault is, that it is begun too early for why torment a boy of ten years old with rules of grammar which he cannot comprehend? why oblige him so early to get any thing by rote, or repeat words to which he can affix no ideas? the memory ought to be exercised, but only in proportion as the judgment ripens: let parents and teachers then watch the progress of a boy's opening apprehension, and adapt their instructions to his slow and gradual improvement, and when he is arrived at an age to comprehend the meaning and force of words, let him use a dictionary, and a plain, simple grammar, to shew him only the inflexions of the different verbs; thus he will arrive, by slow and easy degrees, to comprehend the force of an author, and if he does not attend to all the niceties of a language no longer in use, he will only be defective in what hundreds, with much search and study, have never arrived at: to comprehend the force and spirit of the antient authors is all that is requisite for a knowledge of men and things; to enter into the minutiæ of dead languages, is at best but a fruitless search after words. The passions are the great disturbers of the world, yet their influence on human actions is so mixed and blended with that of the judgment, that it is hardly possible to separate them entirely; nor is it easy for men, at all times, to perceive when they are actuated by the one, and when by the other; to do this distinctly is the principal part of wisdom, and when this knowledge is acquired, the world may be at peace, perhaps it will never be so entirely: education and government are the only means of controling their operation; the latter may restrain them from fear; the former, when rightly conducted, submits them to the restraint of principle, and lessens their pernicious effects, by the cultivation of the heart and faculties. To obtain these two great objects, in any great degree, is perhaps impossible in the present state of society, particularly in the two extremes of riches and poverty. The poor have

have no education, the rich have hardly any; whoever will examine attentively these two different ranks, will find, that this is not hastily asserted. The former, if by chance they are sent to school, can there only be taught to read and write, but if they are corrected, either there or at home, it can only be as the passions of their parents or teachers suggest, without any idea of their amendment; a hasty blow, or harsh word, are the common correctives for all dispositions, and for all faults. No pains are taken, nor can be taken, to check the rising propensities to evil, nor promote a disposition to virtue; indulgence, or correction, equally violent, are all they experience, and of all extremes these are the most dangerous; the first makes them tyrants, the second slaves: to be honest from principle, they are never taught, for fear is a more powerful motive, and better suited to the strength of their temptations; and if this restrains them from the commission of enormous crimes, it is all that can be expected: a poor man thinks it little sin to steal from a rich one, when he can do it with secrecy, and this we need not wonder at in a world in which they have so few
com-

comforts. We will now turn to the other extreme, and see whether the education of the rich any better promotes the two objects above-mentioned. Surrounded on every side by the pleasures, the pursuits, and the temptations which riches afford, they have no leisure to attend to their children, who are therefore committed entirely, in their infancy, to hirelings: the extremes of severity and indulgence, which lead to tyranny and vice, they are equally subject to, from the unrestrained passions of their parents; the former destroys the spirit, and quenches every spark of generosity, for he who has once been a slave, will be a tyrant when he can; and he who has early been accustomed to excessive indulgence, is unprepared for disappointments and difficulties, so that by each extreme the heart is debased and corrupted, and a rich man, who is hardened either by ignorance or design against the miseries of his fellow creatures, is a pest to society, for such a man is bound not only to relieve the pressing necessities of the poor by the precarious supply of occasional alms, but by a constant attention to their moral as well as their temporal wants, to improve their condition

dition in civilifed fociety, and render them fatisfied with their ftation by the comforts they enjoy; but can we expect all this from men who have been taught to confider the poor as a different race of beings from themfelves, born and fupported folely for their ufe and luxury? Impoffible! till the rich are early taught to reftrain their paffions,—till they ceafe to confider all that is given to the poor as taken from their own enjoyment,—till they are early inftructed in principles of juftice, truth, and benevolence, it is needlefs to expect any great improvement in the ftate of fociety; " *men do not gather grapes of thorns,* " *nor figs of thiftles ;*" the means and the end muft be proportioned: but though I have fpoken thus feverely of the two extremes of fociety, yet I by no means deny that there are bright exceptions in both; but thefe being no more than accidental inftances of good difpofitions and great talents, rifing fuperior to fuch powerful difadvantages, form no argument againft the principles I have advanced: now, as this fubject is of confiderable importance, I will extend my refearches a little further, and offer fome remarks on the inftruction of children at an earlier period,

riod. Whether there is any natural difference in the faculties and difpofitions of children, is a point no longer difputed, for there can be none. Mr Locke has proved, that there are no fuch things as innate ideas, as all our ideas are acquired only from external objects; therefore the minds and tempers of children can only be influenced by thofe things which furround them; but as this muft be in a manner almoft imperceptible in early years, particularly when it is little attended to, we are apt to fuppofe that thefe effects are produced not by external caufes, but by certain natural difpofitions which children bring into the world with them; how far a particular formation of body may influence the difpofition of the mind, and difpofe them to be differently affected by external objects, fo as to produce a particular fpecies of talent or of temper, it is almoft impoffible to determine; but certain it is, that there can be no previous difpofition of the mind before the birth of a child: the minds of children, after their birth, grow with their bodies; they muft therefore, in fome meafure, be influenced by the texture of the body, but how or in what degree, can never perhaps be determined;

for

for though two children should be placed in situations as nearly similar as possible, yet there will be a difference in these children's dispositions and talents; this, therefore, must depend on some particular formation of the body and nerves: now over this we have no control, but over those external events and accidents which influence the dispositions of children we certainly have some power; and it is the duty of every parent to attend minutely to the manner in which they operate on the temper and mental faculties of his child, for by these their future character in life is frequently determined, and so strong is the effect of these, that even men, after their temper and talents seem to be completely formed, may be altered for the better or the worse, according to particular events which may happen to them at different periods. Among the many things which contribute to affect the characters of children, the most minute should be attended to; the influence of external objects, in their early years, may have produced such a difference in their dispositions, as to require an entirely different treatment; pain and sickness, for instance, may have effects which are not immediately

mediately perceived: before children have arrived at an age to distinguish between right and wrong, and to be talked to with any effect, it is difficult to know how to correct them, whether by gentle or severe means; it is certain they will understand and remember the effect of a whipping better than all that can be said to them, yet this is a dangerous remedy, because it may have such an influence on their tempers as to be required even after their judgment is come to greater maturity, and thus implant in them habits of fear or obstinacy: when parents are anxious to attend to every thing which concerns their children, they will be able to judge according to what they see and feel to be right; few methods, either of mildness or severity, can apply strictly to all cases: it is only by a minute attention to minute differences, that the conduct of parents to their children can be regulated; but though in the management of children there are many things which must be left to the direction of parents, to act according as they think right, yet there are some general principles which are equally applicable to all. The first thing to which a child should be habituated, is to speak

speak truth, but then parents should do the same; without this, the other is of no use, for when they find it out, they will despise you, and become liars themselves: there are many apparently innocent deceptions to which people accustom themselves towards their children, yet all these have their effect imperceptibly; for instance, if a child falls, and is hurt, the parent to soothe him, tells him he has hurt the floor, which naturally teaches the child to be unfeeling, by making him think his own pain can be lessened by the pains of another. Some people not less foolishly tell the child to beat the floor for hurting him: " a naughty floor to hurt my " poor boy," is generally the exclamation of a foolish parent: tell the child at once to be patient, and endeavor to amuse his attention by something else, and you will by degrees enable him to bear bodily pain with firmness and fortitude: never in any instance deceive a child, for in time you may expect that he will deceive you; teach him to know things as they are, and he will always act on principles of truth and simplicity, for a child early accustomed to be deceived, naturally acquires habits of deceit and fraud. I have heard it considered

considered as an excellent maxim, never to give up to a child what you have once refused; but I think this ought not to be done in all instances, because it tends to dispirit a child, and to make him believe, that in life, what he cannot obtain easily must be given up, than which nothing can be more pernicious; we ought rather to teach him to believe that any thing may be obtained by perseverance. Teach them early to make distinctions, and avoid extremes. Let children early be accustomed to do all they can for themselves, constant attendance depraves their minds and weakens their bodies; let them seldom have any thing they cry for, by this means they will be habituated to disappointment; yet too frequent and needless severity sours their tempers, and engenders hatred and dislike, rather than filial piety. Never bribe them by any thing but praise, all other rewards tend to make them mercenary and grossly corrupt; no motive of action is so pure as the love of applause, all others degrade and enslave. Let them never be taught to despise any other children because they are poorer than themselves, but to pity them because they have not had equal advantages.

tages. Till they can comprehend the nature and difference of things, let them submit from the feelings of superiority; after that, teach them the true grounds of submission, which is, that such and such things are not proper to be had, because they belong to another, or are too expensive, &c. Never threaten a child with what you never intend to do, for by that means they will in time despise your threats, and have no fixed rule of conduct; when they are sure the punishment will follow the offence, they will be cautious how they offend. To children who are turned two or three years, I should by no means advise any corporal punishment to be used, if it can possibly be avoided, for it serves only to render them hardened, or servile, or timorous; any punishment which applies to the mental feelings is much better suited to promote virtuous and moral dispositions, the other is suited only to the most abject slaves. Let children early be taught to respect the distinction between *meum* and *tuum*, what is their own, and what belongs to others; the want of attending to this occasions most of the miseries of the world: never let them cry for what does not belong to them,

them, nor endeavor to take it from others. Teach them early to be generous, and part easily with any thing they have, and always take what you desire them to give, for without this it becomes in time a mere form, and when it is taken they are vexed and disappointed. Let great pains be taken to strengthen and exercise their bodies, as well as their minds, for by so doing you afford them constant sources of amusement, and let all their sports have a reference to something useful, for the more they are amused innocently, the more they will be preserved from vicious indulgences. Never be severe with children about trifles, it renders them unhappy, and consequently fretful and peevish, a few foibles and a few faults may be passed over without much danger: "be not ex-"treme to mark what is done amiss," may serve as an admonition as well as a prayer; a lenient indulgence to the foibles of young people is often the truest wisdom; the youth that might have been reclaimed by lenity and forgiveness, may be lost by severity, and from levity may with hasty strides, sink into hopeless depravity. The ideas of men are all acquired,—much therefore

fore depends on what they are taught; the savage is the emblem of the child, he has no means of instruction, and remains a child all his life, with no other ideas than the first objects which strike his sight can convey: man is entirely a creature of art, for a child left alone in a desart will, when he is arrived at the age of eight or ten years, be found dirty, indolent, cruel, ignorant, jealous, passionate, and revengeful; he will not have the speech of man, and it is doubtful whether he will always walk upright: we should view man in all his gradations, from this state to his present point of refinement, to be satisfied how much he is indebted to instruction and society: from all this it is evident how much depends on what children are early taught; it is therefore of the utmost consequence that they are taught what is right.

UNION WITH IRELAND.

" I write in Great Britain, and direct
" my thoughts for this kingdom, wishing
" for *peace, tranquillity, and union* between the
" two Islands. (July 1797.)" p. 323. The author's wish is completed, and the two nations, after many a reluctant struggle on the
part

part of Ireland, are at length united: whether the fruits of this unequal union will be as was pretended and expected, tranquillity and prosperity, time, which is the mother of truth, alone can determine; ministers, on this occasion, seem to have adopted the maxim of the old lady, in her advice to her daughter—" Marry first, and love will come " after;" it is a dangerous experiment, but frequently tried. A little like most fashionable matches, this late Irish wedding has been brought about, more from interest than from any cordial love on either side; and in such cases, happiness is neither expected nor deserved: the pretended friends and relations of the parties seem to be the only people concerned, and if they gratify themselves, it appears to be all that was intended. To speak seriously of this boasted union, I will hazard an opinion which seems to be somewhat hardy, yet, as I believe, fully justified by the state of things. Anxious only for the peace and happiness of mankind, and totally indifferent about forms of government, I have ever viewed the union with Ireland only as the means of promoting the prosperity of the two countries, of healing all religious and
political

political differences, and providing for the permanent interest of both parties; should it produce these effects, I will never regret the means that have been used for its attainment, and forgetting all that is past, rejoice in the present, and look for increasing happiness: but I will honestly confess, that I expect no such consequences; on the contrary, when Ireland has gained a little strength, which she may after a few years of tranquillity, I fully expect to see the union end in final separation and enmity, if the two countries are not earlier torn asunder by some ruder and more sudden accident.

THE ALBIGENSES.

" The Albigenses were a sect of the Wal-
" denses, who had their rise in the twelfth
" century." p. 323. The author's short note, shews that he is not much acquainted either with the history or the principles of these unfortunate reformers. The most exact and authentic account of them is to be found in a set of Tracts, published in 1612, by Gretzer, a German Jesuit. Among these, the most remarkable is that of Rinieri, or as it is latinifed, Reinerus, an Italian Inquisitor,

but at one time a member of the sect of the Waldenses; and as all apostates think it requisite to convince their new friends of their sincerity by their violence, he seems to have been inflamed with a laudable zeal against his former companions, and to have recommended and enforced various methods to get rid of them by fire, and sword, and torture. Another incentive to this pious apostate was the hope of an Archbishopric, but his ambitious designs were suddenly destroyed by Uberto Pallavicino, who condemned him to banishment, in which state he died a miserable example of disappointed ambition, and a warning to all traitors. The following are among the crimes of the Waldenses, as related by their Persecutor, Rinieri—" They
" denied the church of Rome to be the
" church of Christ, which they said, it ceased
" to be under Pope Sylvester, for then it first
" began to acquire temporal property; they
" called the Pope Antichrist, and his bishops
" murderers, on account of their wars and
" persecutions; they refused to pay tithes,
" and esteemed it sinful to endow churches
" and monasteries; they condemned the
" clergy for their idle lives, and disregarded
" all

" all the privileges and ceremonies of the
" church; they denied its sacraments, and
" derided its festivals, esteeming all days
" alike; baptism of infants they held to be
" of no avail, and denied the right of a priest
" to confer the eucharist, saying that they
" communicate daily, while they remember
" Christ in their lives; they denied the ne-
" cessity of priests, saying, that every good
" layman is a priest inasmuch as the apostles
" were laymen, and that every man and
" woman may preach; they condemned the
" use of the Latin tongue in the service of
" the church; they knew most of the old
" testament by heart; they believed in no
" saints but the apostles, and prayed to none
" but God; they had no litany, believed no
" legends of the saints, and laughed at all
" their miracles; they affirmed, that male-
" factors ought not to be punished with
" death, and said, that all ecclesiastical judg-
" ments were intended, not for correction,
" but to gratify avarice." Here follow the
marks by which these heretics were to be
found out, from whence it may be seen how
far removed from primitive christianity they
must have been, who could consider such

simplicity of faith and manners as unworthy of a chriſtian community. "Firſt," ſays Rinieri, "they may be perceived by their
"manners and their words; they ſhew no
"pride in dreſs, for their cloaths are neither
"coſtly nor ornamented; the affairs of the
"world they avoid, for fear of lies, and
"oaths, and frauds; their teachers are cob-
"lers and weavers: they do not multiply
"riches, and are content with little wealth;
"they are chaſte and temperate, and ſeldom
"pray; they go to church under pretence
"of religion, but in truth only to entrap the
"preacher in his words; they avoid ſcurri-
"lity, and levity of ſpeech, and lying, and
"ſwearing; they inſinuate themſelves into
"the acquaintance of the rich and noble by
"the following means—they expoſe to ſale
"ſuch things as are likely to tempt them to
"buy, for inſtance, rings and laces, and when
"they have ſold theſe, ſhould their cuſtom-
"ers aſk them if they have any thing elſe to
"ſell, they anſwer that they have more pre-
"cious goods than theſe, if they will promiſe
"not to betray them to the prieſts; ſecurity
"being pledged, they then ſay, 'I have to
"ſhew you a bright gem, the gift of God,
"by

"by which a man may become acquainted
"with his Maker;' the pedlar then recites
"to them such texts as these—" *The scribes
"sit in Moses's seat,*"—"*Wo unto them that take
"the key of knowledge,*" &c.—and being asked
"to whom they apply these, they say, " To
"the Romish clergy:" they then enter into
"a comparison between themselves and
"the priests.—" The teachers of the church
"of Rome," say they, " are pompous in
"their dress and manners, they love the
"chief seats in synagogues, and to be called
"Rabbi, Rabbi, but we require no such
"titles; they are unchaste, but each of us
"has his own wife, and lives contented with
"her; they are rich and covetous, and to
"them it is said, " *Wo unto you rich,*" we hav-
"ing food and raiment, are therewith con-
"tent: they are voluptuous, and unto them
"it is said, " *Wo unto you which devour widows'
"houses,*" we live as we can: they wage war,
"and plunder the poor, and to them it is
"said, " *He that taketh up the sword must perish
"by the sword,*" we endure persecution from
"them for righteousness' sake; they eat idle
"bread, we work with our own hands;
"they desire to be the only teachers, with us
"both

"both men and women teach; they have
"more regard for the traditions of men than
"the commands of God, as to fasts and
"feasts, and many other things, which are
"mere human institutions; they load their
"penitents with punishments, we, after the
"example of Christ, say, "*Go thy way, and
"sin no more;*" we remit all sins, and send
"the soul to heaven, they send all souls to
"hell." "Thus," says Rinieri, "is the faith
"corrupted, and destroyed." This pious
persecutor of the Waldenses, after thus bearing testimony to the purity of their doctrines, acknowledges their extensive propagation.
"There is no land," says he, "which has
"been free from them at some time or
"other." Having said thus much, he proceeds to enumerate six causes of their heresy; but he seems sometimes to confound causes with effects. "The first," says he, "is vain-
"glory; secondly, their zeal in making con-
"verts, for both men and women teach, by
"day and by night, and so rapid is the pro-
"ficiency of their converts, that the novice
"of three days begins to teach others. To
"those who excuse themselves, by saying
"they cannot learn, they say, 'learn but a
"word

" word a day, and you will know three hun-
" dred and fixty-five in the year.' What I
" am going to affirm, is true. A certain he-
" retic, defirous to pervert his neighbour
" from the faith, fwam to him by night
" acrofs the Ibis, in the depth of winter: the
" third caufe of herefy, is their having tranf-
" lated the New Teftament into the vulgar
" tongue, and teaching it the people, which
" they do with all poffible fecrecy, for fear of
" the priefts: the fourth is the diffolute lives
" of fome of the clergy: the fifth is the infuf-
" ficiency of the doctrines of many of our
" preachers: the fixth, the irreverence with
" which fome of our minifters treat the fa-
" craments of our church: and the feventh"
(here he forgets that he promifed to mention
only fix) " is their hatred of the clergy;
" for," fays he, " I have heard many of thefe
" heretics fay, that they wifh to reduce the
" clergy to the ftate of hedgers and ditchers,
" by taking away their tythes and church
" property." To root out fuch dangerous
heretics, no mode of perfecution and terror
was omitted by Emperors, Popes, and Bi-
fhops; it is of no ufe to enumerate them, as
they may be eafily conceived. At what time
this

this herefy firft arofe, it is now difficult to determine, yet whether they owe their origin to Peter Waldo, a citizen of Lyons, or they are to be looked for many years earlier in the vallies of Italy, is now a matter of little confequence; but the reformers of later times are proud to claim a kindred to them, and affert, that they exifted foon after the times of the Apoftles. Though nearly exterminated by Frederick the 2d of Germany, they ftill, like the phœnix, rofe from their afhes, and flourifhed in various places, for their zeal in making converts was equal to their fortitude in fuffering; after a dreadful perfecution in France, under the name of Albigenfes, they fuffered again in the vallies of Italy, in the time of Oliver Cromwell; he fent Sir Samuel Moreland with a confiderable fum of money to their relief, who publifhed an account of his miffion in his hiftory of the evangelical churches in Italy; he was * a good mechanic, having invented many ufeful machines, but a bad politician, and a worfe writer.

EPIC

---

* See Grainger's Hiftory of England.

EPIC POETRY.

"He gave the publick a long quarto volume of epick verses, JOAN OF ARC, written, as he says in the preface, in *six weeks.*" p. 353. There are three epic poems in the world, and there will never be another. Homer, Virgil, and Milton, need fear no future rivals. All the receipts of the critics have never yet produced an epic poet; they may enable others to judge of their merits; they may direct the efforts of genius, but they can never supply the want of it; for poetry is the gift of nature, rules are the result of art. The great fault of modern epic poetry, is the frequent appearance of the poet, particularly in drawing characters. Homer never draws a character; Voltaire never introduces a hero without giving his own opinion of him; so that he no longer writes a poem but a history. A painter, who, at the bottom of his picture, should write the character or passion he meant to express, must be thought ridiculous; and a poet is no less so, who does not leave the characters of his heroes to be drawn by the reader. An epic poet ought to represent the man, not to describe him; and if his language and animation are not sufficient to set his characters before us, it is in vain he attempts to labor them, the illusion is destroyed; and, instead of a poet, he becomes only an historian. This distinction will be found to apply constantly.

HORNE TOOKE.

" Mr. HORNE TOOKE, in the conclusion
" of his " Diversions of Purley," makes an
" apology for applying himself to subjects so
" trivial as grammatical discussions, in the
" year 1786. He uses the words of an
" Italian poet, which are very remarkable,
" though they never have been much no-
" ticed." p. 353. To the extensive learning, acuteness, ingenuity, humor, fortitude, and integrity of Mr Horne Tooke, it is not in my power to do justice, yet as a tribute of gratitude for his unrivalled exertions in the public service, I will attempt to redeem his character from the odium which it has suffered even with well-intentioned men, through the interested misrepresentations of the hirelings of power, and the slavish advocates of established authority; from such

inveterate

inveterate enemies a good man is seldom safe in his life time,—posterity only can do him justice. In answer to all those who have branded him with the appellations of turbulent, seditious, pestilent, troublesome, and contentious, I will only answer, that his whole life is unstained by a single act of baseness, yet a man who is determined to be the unceasing enemy of corruption, must lead a turbulent and a troublesome life; but that Mr Tooke has not been actuated by the mere love of contention is evident from his having been the friend of ministry while a hope remained of their being the friends of reform; for the truth of this, I refer to his famous *Two Pair of Portraits*. That he has been equally the enemy of ministers and opposition is a proof of his own sincerity, because he has nothing to hope from either, and no disgrace to a man who sees that the objects of both are the same, though accident has placed them differently. That he is not sincere and in earnest can hardly be objected to a man who has suffered, more than once, a rigorous imprisonment, and been once tried for his life. That his objects are undefined, boundless, and vague, is unjustly alledged against a man who has published a specific plan of reform, from which he has never been known at any time to deviate. That he has ever sought the wages of corruption, though it has been asserted, has never been proved. That he has been the means of overturning certain political societies to which he has belonged, is false, if asserted generally; and where it is true, he has deserved praise rather than blame, for when the society of the Bill of Rights so far forget the ends of its institution as to make the payment of a certain great patriot's debts the first object of its regard, it was time that the public should be undeceived; and it is to the credit of Mr Tooke's talents, as well as his integrity, that he was both able and willing to bring such a society to an untimely death. That he was the means of introducing disunion into another society*, was likewise to his credit; he put the temper of some of its members to the test, and shewed that they were not actuated by any desire of promoting the public good, but merely meant to distress the ministers; such men he has at all times delighted to expose, for his penetration pierces through every

* The Friends of the People.

every difguife, and fuch is their weaknefs, that they have given him frequent opportunities: Junius is not the only falfe patriot who fuffered from his fearching feverity. That he has laughed in fecret, and even openly, at the over-heated zeal of fome reformers, is not to be wondered at in a man who has a talent for humor; but that he has ever ferioufly acted a double part, by pretending to be interefted for what he has no regard, is a fuppofition which fhews little knowledge of him, or of human nature; he has given too many proofs of his fincerity to have it rafhly doubted: to fome people this defence may feem needlefs, but I have heard all that I have anfwered, and more, faid againft him, in various companies, and by fome people who wifhed to think well of him, by others who never think at all, and by more who are determined to think ill of him; fuch is the power of detraction, fo unwilling are the generality of men to refift eftablifhed corruptions, and fo inured to deceit that they can with difficulty believe any man honeft: after this general anfwer to all his defamers, it is needlefs to fay any thing

thing particularly to repel our author's wicked asperity.

REFORM.

" The state of Europe has PROVED the intentions of France from the first moment of her Revolution; and every historical document daily confirms the proof." p. 359. The enemies of reform have but one argument left, (and they do well to bring it forward whenever the question is publicly agitated) viz. the French Revolution. But this argument, like that of all men who are driven to difficulties, is derived from the perversion of a principle, not simply from the exercise of it; and, as they use it, might apply against a reform in Turkey as well as in Great-Britain. The fallacy of the argument consists in not stating the difference between a reform proceeding from a government, and one forced upon it; as for instance, in the difference between the English Revolution in 1688, and the subsequent century. Reform neglected leads to revolution and anarchy: yet, after all that can be said, there is, without doubt, a certain fatality incident to nations as well as individuals,

dividuals, which leads them to their ruin against all wisdom and argument.

ELOQUENCE.

" But *such as it is*, eloquence in the politi-
" cal world is like charity in the Christian
" character; without it a man is counted
" dead." p. 363. Among all the talents with which man, either by nature or by art is furnished, there seems none to me more questionable in its effects than eloquence, yet some men deny that it ever produced any good effect to the public in those times in which it is allowed most to have flourished: the eloquence of Demosthenes was ineffectual to save his country from ruin, and though Cicero inflamed the senate against the crimes of Catiline, he could not restrain the violence of Antony. Juvenal has recorded the vanity of eloquence,* and remarked, that it caused the death of its two greatest ornaments. Demosthenes has left us nothing but his orations: if those of Cicero were lost, we might still consider him as one of the greatest men of his time; his moral

* Eloquio sed uterque perit orator.
Sat. x. 114.

moral and critical works will for ever enlighten and improve mankind, but his orations might cease to be read without much danger. Eloquence is a talent which may be turned to any purpose, it may paint the blessings of liberty in the most glowing and attractive colors, but it may also disguise the horrors of slavery, and reconcile men, by its impressive power, to the worst evils of injustice and tyranny. Eloquence is oftener needed to perplex the truth than to enforce it, for truth will always shine by its own intrinsic lustre, while error requires the borrowed light of eloquence to shine at all; truth can never ultimately be concealed, nor error long prevail without the aid of foreign ornament: eloquence has done more to mislead mankind than to enlighten them, for it has not often fallen to the lot of those who have conferred the greatest services on their country. The base flatterers of Philip exhausted their seducing eloquence to lull their country into a fatal repose during the machinations of the tyrant, and even the oratory of Isocrates was misapplied to the same iniquitous purpose. The talents for speaking and acting seem so totally distinct, that they are
seldom

seldom found united in the same man: the greatest statesmen in our own country have been no orators; and it may safely be added, that the greatest orators, with one single exception, have been no statesmen. Though a fine speech is unfortunately considered in our times as the summit of human wisdom, yet all the eloquence of Mr Fox has never added a single vote to his party, nor all the talents of his antagonist produced one measure of wisdom, foresight, or sound policy; so little has eloquence to do with the prosperity or happiness of a country. Eloquence is generally addressed to the passions, while the calmer researches of philosophy apply only to the judgment; the orator glories in hurrying men along, without giving them time to consider whither they are going, or where they are to stop, or to examine whether he is right or wrong; but the glory of the philosopher rests on surer ground, he delights to appeal to the judgment, rather than to the feelings, and consults posterity, rather than the present moment; he addresses his ideas to the public, and submits them to the severest examination and reproof; the orator addresses only a particular circle, and to serve a momentary purpose, and his orations are seldom calculated to bear a strict examination, as to their intrinsic merit or force of argument. Eloquence has, on the whole, contributed little to improve and civilize mankind, for its effects are fleeting and transitory; but the patient efforts of the moralist are permanent, sure, and steady. Eloquence is like arbitrary power; when in the hands of an honest man, it is capable of conferring the greatest happiness on society, by protecting the innocent, succoring the distressed, defending virtue, promoting the arts, and punishing vice and immorality. Eloquence is the most dangerous gift to be entrusted to man, because the misuse of it is attended with evils more numerous than its most noble exertions are capable of producing good; it places one man so much in the power of another, or rather whole nations in the power of one man, that without that man is endowed with the best dispositions, to the rest of society, he is capable of injuring them in the dearest interests, and overturning the greatest privileges they have ever enjoyed.

INFIDELS.

"Read the Memoires of the Abbe BA-
"RUEL, and doubt, if you can, whether LI-
"TERATURE has power to kill, and to make
"alive." p. 369. The Abbe Baruel, the author of the Purfuits of Literature, and the whole train of Anti-Jacobin writers, have been at great pains to connect the literature of France, and the horrors of the French Revolution, yet they have failed in their attempt, in the opinion of all honeft and impartial men, for fuch eafily perceive that they are no more connected than the cruelties which have been committed in the name of religion are to be attributed to the mild and amiable precepts of the author of chriftianity. Though I do not mean to leffen the horror which any pious believer may entertain of atheifm and infidelity, nor his habitual veneration for the Bible and the Book of Common Prayer, yet I am anxious to do juftice to the intentions of thofe men who thought they acted wifely in fo doing, and miftook for prejudices in others, what they were not fo fortunate as to believe. The cruelties which have, at various times, been

been committed for the support and propagation of christianity, no one will deny to be contrary both to its language and spirit, for the words of its Divine Teacher are express to the purpose,—" *He that useth the sword, shall perish by the sword.*" Now, if the writings of the infidels expressly condemn all violence, persecution, and cruelty, and contain every where sentiments of universal benevolence, toleration, and mercy, is it not equally unjust to impute to them the crimes which have been committed under pretence of propagating their principles, as it is to impute to Christ and his apostles the persecutions of kings, popes, and emperors, committed in the name of christianity? no inference can be more unjust, it is therefore only honest to acquit men of what they never intended; it may be said, that though they were innocent, yet they were ignorant, and that though they did not intend evil, yet that it was the natural consequence of their principles: though this is no more true in the one case than the other; the fact is, that the crimes were committed in both cases, by men who never thought about principles in either; they were committed by men who, having no other

other objects than ambition and the love of power, are always ready to take advantage of the confusion which all great changes of opinion create in the theatre of the world, and call themselves atheists or christians, just as it suits their purpose.

PROFESSOR HEYNE.

"Professor Heyne was originally a mecha-
"nick: he was not born with taste, and he
"never acquired elegance. His learning is
"without discernment. More embodied
"dulness, or a heavier mass of matter than
"*his* Virgil I never saw. The shrine of the
"Poet is indeed loaded with offerings, but it
"is illuminated with rays from Gottingen."
p. 389. Surely it can be no just reproach to Professor Heyne, in the estimation of any liberal man, that he was originally bred a mechanic, the same might be said of many other very learned men, and said to their credit, if their talents or industry have promoted them beyond their original destination and lot; some men can neither advance themselves, nor keep their place in society. To say that he was not born with taste, is no more than might be said of every other man;
and

and he has made little advance in the knowledge of human nature: who supposes any of our intellectual faculties born with us? he might as well suppose us to come into the world with them arrived at full and complete maturity. That Professor Heyne has never acquired elegance, is no reproach to him, yet certainly a misfortune to his readers, for his Latin is worse than that of any modern editor, the great Brunck not excepted; his notes are trifling, and his dissertations dull and tedious. I should be sorry to see any other classic fall into his hands; and, I trust, the race of such heavy critics is nearly extinct; we have need of a revolution in classical literature, if it is not needed elsewhere, for there are few editions of the classics suited to general readers; to men who study the antient authors, for the matter, not for the words they contain, and are therefore not nice about a minute difference of expressions, provided they comprehend the general force of an author's meaning and sentiments. The present editions of Greek and Latin authors are either loaded with a tiresome succession of verbal criticisms, or a pompous display of useless erudition, which fatigue without in-

forming

forming the reader, and are more suited to excite weariness and disgust, than to elucidate or improve. All that is wanted is a pure, well-settled text, a solution of grammatical difficulties, and an explanation of such passages as contain remote or historical allusions, or such other particulars as are requisite to a compleat knowledge of the meaning and force of the author who is undertaken to be published; such is the duty of an editor who wishes to be useful, rather than to display his own treasures.

NATIONAL BANKRUPTCY.

"A REVOLUTION IS NOT THE NECESSARY CONSEQUENCE OF BANKRUPTCY." p. 432. Though the author of the Pursuits of Literature may think so, I should be sorry to try the experiment, for whenever the great fabric of paper falls, it will crush us all in its ruins. The merchant, the manufacturer, the sailor, the soldier, the landed proprietor, and the stock-holder, all depend on each other, and the whole on the credit of our trade, for the landed property of the nation is mortgaged for more than double its worth. The case of the nation is that of a gentleman

tleman of good landed estate who mortgages that estate for double its amount, and employs the money in trade, which enables him to pay the interest of his debt, and live handsomely on the remainder; as long as his expences bear any proportion to the surplus of his gains, so long he may go on safely, but when his utmost exertions in trade are unable to procure him any further credit, the consequence is evident, the gentleman's affairs will be thrown into confusion, his hirelings and dependents will desert him, and seek elsewhere, and by other means, to gain a subsistence.

UNIVERSAL PEACE.

" The most ardent wish of my heart is A
" SECURE PEACE, after a war for ever to be
" deplored, bloody, fatal, and expensive be-
" yond all example; but which I always
" believed, and still believe, to have been
" INEVITABLE." p. 439. The sentiments and expectations of the loudest advocates for war are now much softened by adversity. The events of nine unsuccessful campaigns against liberty, have taught them, that a nation, determined to be free, can never be subdued,

dued, and they now renounce the chimerical project of imposing a government upon France; security is all they pretend to aim at, and that security might have been more easily and cheaply obtained from an infant republic than from one rooted and consolidated by nine years of victorious warfare, and invigorated by the affections of the people, and the wisdom of its rulers; yet there can be no peace till both parties are convinced of the sincerity of each other. So much for the present war, which some think will be the last of any consequence. Should I venture to hazard an opinion on the probability of that future reign of peace, which many benevolent writers have delighted to contemplate, I should say, that at some yet distant period, when the spirit of wisdom is more extensively diffused, and the possession of property more equally divided, it is not impossible that men may see the folly of fighting other people's battles, and be no longer seduced or compelled to risque their lives for the means of living or the less justifiable motives of national vanity, or national revenge; that the evil passions will ever be wholly eradicated from the human breast, so as to make the world what it has never yet been, a terrestrial paradise, is by no means probable, we ought then indeed to alter the nature of man, and have, as it has been sneeringly suggested, on the supposition of extirpating war, a new Adam and a new Eve; but that men should cease to risque their lives, to gratify people's passions, is neither unnatural nor improbable; whenever this happens, the rulers of the world will then consider the interest of individuals simply as such, and not sacrifice one part of the nation for the good of the remainder. The time will come, I have no doubt, when the idea of two nations going to war will be thought as ridiculous as it is now that they should live at peace with each other.

Tunc genus humanum positis sibi consulat armis
In que vicem gens omnis amet.

Lucan. lib. i. l. 60.

The ambition and quarrels of individuals have, in all ages, been the origin of wars, and the people have ever been the sufferers; we do not wonder, among barbarous nations, at the frequency or severity of their contests,

yet

yet after the arts and habits of civilization have been introduced and extended, that the occupation of a soldier should find a place, and fighting become a trade, is an anomaly no otherwise to be accounted for, than by supposing that civilization is not yet complete, and that the rights of society are not yet equally enjoyed.

PATRIOTS.

" I have walked in the school of Locke, " and have passed through that of Sidney." p. 443. This sentence is equally false, and conceited. Let not the names of these great men be profaned by such an alliance, to such men as these the world is indebted for all that it at present enjoys of liberty, virtue, and happiness; for had not they hazarded their lives and comfort, and patiently endured the world's contempt, darkness might yet have overspread the face of the earth, and the moral world been without form or comeliness. To those purer souls who, refined from the gross feelings of interest and servility, have written, fought, and suffered for their country, it is owing that the glorious flame of liberty has been kept alive in the earth, and the mafs of fociety preferved from corruption and rottennefs; for without liberty every other gift of heaven is dull and fpiritlefs: what are knowledge, wealth, or talents, without the power to ufe them freely and honorably? what are friends and honors, without fecure enjoyment? what is even life without liberty? To thofe then who have furrendered their own comfort and quiet, to fecure this ineftimable bleffing, to their own age and to pofterity, the world is indebted as its beft benefactors; and though they feemed to fuffer in their lives, by the facrifices they made of eafe and comfort, yet they had pleafures which the fordid fons of corruption can never feel; they had pleafures which men of common clay can never tafte—they had their reward in the pure and animated enjoyment of having done a fervice to the world which no narrow confiderations of private intereft can ever equal, and narrow fouls can never comprehend. Let us then erect altars, and raife ftatues to the memory of thofe illuftrious patriots who have fuftained the caufe of liberty by their

pen,

pen, their sword, or their purse; yet if public gratitude should fail to honor them with due respect, their memory will still live in the breast of every honest man, who prizes his liberty dearer than his existence, yet may they never cease to be had in public remembrance!

NOTES.

NOTES.

Vide p. 5. The interesting work of Madame de Stael, " De la Literature dans ses rapports avec les Institutions " Sociales," deserves to be read with particular attention, as it developes the causes of past, and the means of future improvement, and appreciates, with force and judgment, the merits of the antients, compared with the moderns; it is a work of profound reflection, and written with uncommon brilliancy; there are some mistakes as to historical facts, but few errors of opinion or sentiment.

Vide p. 11. A certain popular writer on morality, Dr Paley, has, in my opinion, very wisely omitted to rest morality on any other ground than general utility, for no actions can be right or wrong independent of their consequences. Benevolence is a virtue only because it is found to promote happiness, and fornication is a vice only because it produces private and general misery.

Vide p. 13. The apostolic succession, to which both papist and protestant bishops appeal, as the origin of their dignity, seems to me, after the fullest examination, to belong only to the presbyterians, for till the commencement of the second century, no such persons were known as bishops; the apostles, it is true, were called επισκοποι, or overseers of the churches they had planted, but after their decease, we every
where

where find thefe churches governed by prefbyters, elected by the people, till the fecond century. The whole epiftle of St Clement, the firft in date and importance after the apoftles, feems to have been written againft a fedition in the Roman Church, which aimed to fubvert the government of the prefbyters, and gratify the ambition of an afpiring individual; the Saint every where appeals to the inftitution of the apoftles, and reproves the rafhnefs of thofe who attempted to innovate. Now, after this, all refts on tradition. The firft ecclefiaftical hiftorian, Eufebius, appeals to no other authority, for he did not write till the middle of the third century.

Vide p. 20. In this exquifite piece of poetry, Akenfide has aimed at an imitation of Pindar's firft Pythian ode, in defcribing the power of mufic; yet he has failed, in his attempt, to reprefent the beautiful image of the eagle, in the concife, expreffive terms of the Grecian bard. Gray has done the fame, and fucceeded better without doubt, yet both have fallen fhort of their model; the υγρον νωτον αωρει, are terms not to be expreffed in Englifh; and every language has terms which cannot be tranflated.

P. 32. The learned Ifaac Cafaubon has furnifhed us with a concife character of all thefe theological difputes. Being at Paris, he vifited the college of the Sorbonne; on coming to a particular chamber, the perfon who attended him remarked to him, that that was the chamber in which the Doctors had difputed for more than four hundred years. "And what have they decided," was his reply.—v. Dict. Hiftorique Francais.

P. 36.

P. 36. Thinking it right to prove what I have advanced respecting the writings of Johnson and Parr, I will give some specimens which I trust will convince my readers of the faults of these two great writers. First, as to the pomposity, words, and manner of Johnson—" Meteors play " their coruscations without prognostic or prediction," False Alarm, p. 1. " Among these men there is often the " vociferation of merriment, but very seldom the tranquil- " lity of chearfulness," Rambler, Nº 53. " Long habits " may *superinduce inability* to deny any desire, or repress, " by superior motives, the *importunities* of any *immediate* " *gratification*, and an *inveterate selfishness* will imagine all " advantages diminished in proportion as they are communi- " cated," Rambler, Nº 64. " He could not long hold out " against hilarity, but after a few months began to relax the " rigid muscles of disciplinarian moroseness," Rambler, Nº " 141. A continual exacerbation of hatred, an unextinguish- " able feud, an incessant reciprocation of mischief, a mutual " vigilance to entrap, and eagerness to destroy," Rambler, " Nº 185. " The attention is recreated by unexpected " facility, and the imagination soothed by incidental excel- " lencies," Rambler, Nº 207. " That which they think " to be too parsimoniously distributed to their own claims, " they will not gratuitously squander upon others," Rambler, Nº 193. The inversions of our language, first introduced by Dr Johnson, are now become so familiar, that they are hardly considered as faults; I will instance only a few, and leave the rest to my reader. " To love excellence is " natural," Life of Cowley, p. 9. Here the common arrangement is inverted, and the infinitive mood begins the sentence. " It is natural to love excellence," is the usual method of placing, but Johnson always affected singularity.

" A

" A Doctor of Physic, however, he was made at Oxford, " in December, 1657," Ditto, p. 15. " Of the Olym- " pic Ode, the beginning is, I think, above the original in " elegance, and below it in strength," Ditto, p. 48. " By " this abruption posterity lost more instruction than de- " light," Ditto, p. 60. " Of triplets in his Davideis he " makes no use, and perhaps did not at first think them " allowable," Ditto, p. 69. " From such prepossessions " Milton seems not to have been free," Life of Milton, p. 127. " How much more he originally intended, or " with what events the action was to be concluded, it is in " vain to conjecture," Life of Butler, p. 182. In some instances, it may be said, that the construction of our language is rendered smoother by these inversions, but in the last, and in many others, this excuse cannot be admitted, for there is a mere change without any improvement. The poverty of Johnson's ideas, as he frequently wrote in haste, is sometimes disguised under a pompous diction and manner, which hide from many the most common-place and trivial thoughts; a few examples will be sufficient to prove that this is not hastily advanced. " Every diffuse and com- " plicated question may be examined by different methods, " upon different principles, and that truth which is easily " found by one investigator, may be missed by another, " equally honest and equally diligent," False Alarm, p. 11. All this means nothing more than that, in all disputes, some people must be right and others wrong. " All govern- " ment supposes subjects, all authority implies obedience," Ditto, p. 12. This is a mere truism, pompously expressed: the whole of this political squib is remarkable for a stiff and aukward turn of writing, and its pompous sophistry of argument. His frequent repetitions of the same ideas will be constantly evident to any man sufficiently acquainted with his works. " To disentangle confusion, and illustrate " obscurity," Observation on the State of Affairs in 1756. " The dictators of their conduct, and the arbiters of their " fate," Ditto. " Violations of treaties, and breach of " faith," Ditto. " Vague and indefinite." The latter of these epithets answers the purpose of both; but this is not the only instance where words are multiplied without multiplying ideas. " Rather live by plunder than by agricul- " ture, and consider war as their best trade." A constant affectation of novelty in his expressions, and a certain pointed quaintness, are faults which, having omitted to mention, I will here produce a few instances of, and these may be sufficient for the present. " We know that a few strokes " of an ax will lop a cedar, but what arts of cultivation can " elevate a shrub?" Rambler, N° 25. " Huddled in the " variety of things, and thrown into the general miscellany " of life," Rambler, N° 2. Reflections on Spring he " calls, " vernal speculations," Ditto, N° 5. " Seeming " possibilities, interstitial spaces, and tumultuous hurries," are conceited and needless epithets, v. Rambler, N° 8. " The train and progeny of subordinate apprehensions and " desires," Ditto. " There is a general succession of " events in which contraries are produced by perpetual vi- " cissitudes," Ditto, N° 21. " The hopeless labor of " uniting heterogeneous ideas, digesting independent hints, " and collecting, into one point, the several rays of borrow- " ed light, emitted often with contrary directions," N° 23. These, and such passages as these, are all replete with affectation, because they express common and familiar ideas in pompous and unusual terms. It now only remains for me to give a few instances of affected point and quaintness.

" Men

" Men who lament nothing but the loss of money, and feel
" nothing but a blow," Rambler, Nº 56. " The grati-
" fication of curiosity rather makes us free from uneasiness
" than confers pleasure; we are more pained by ignorance
" than delighted by instruction," Rambler, Nº 103. This
is pointed, but I doubt it is too hastily asserted. " He that
" is too desirous to be loved will soon learn to flatter,"
Ditto, Nº 104. " The greatest human virtue bears no
" portion to human vanity. We always think ourselves
" better than we are, and are generally desirous that others
" should think us better than we think ourselves. To
" praise us for actions or dispositions which deserve praise,
" is not to confer a kindness, but to pay a tribute," Ditto,
Nº 104. This whole number is remarkable for such
pointed sentences, which have more keenness than truth, or
knowledge of mankind. " Where there is no hope, there
" can be no endeavor. For every single act of progression
" a short time is sufficient, and it is only requisite, that
" whenever that time is afforded it be well employed,"
Ditto, Nº 108. These are a few of the faults of Johnson's
stile, and there are many others which it might not be difficult to point out; his bigotry, superstition, and prejudice
require a fuller examination, which may be given at some
future period. Yet with all his failings, as a writer and a
man, we are infinitely indebted to him for his important services to literature and morality. The language of Dr Parr
has some, but not all the faults of Johnson; he often uses
pompous words, but they are generally forcible, and convey
a strong meaning, while those of Johnson are often used to
disguise very trivial thoughts, and without that precision
and accuracy which are constantly required to convey our
ideas. The only fault of the splendid Dedication to Hurd,

is the too frequent use of epithets, and for this, one passage is remarkable. "It is not arrayed in any delusive resem-
"blance either of solemnity from fanatical cant, of profound-
"ness from scholastic jargon, of precision from the crabbed
"formalities of cloudy philologists, or of refinement from
"the technical babble of frivolous connoisseurs." This perhaps is the only passage in the whole which is thoroughly reprehensible, the rest is in the grandest stile of dignity and elevation; it is exquisitely and splendidly finished, and it is impossible to produce more brilliant passages from any work in the English language, Junius, who is our best writer, not excepted. "These are lucky situations in which it pushes at
"once from the dim and tremulous twilight of uncertainty
"to the full and steady brightness of conviction," Remarks on the Statement of Dr Combe. This is pompous and affected. "What I thought of Mr Fox has been else-
"where stated, and I continue to think the same with in-
"creased conviction." So far is well, and intelligible.
"Great as may be my admiration of that man, when sur-
"veyed on the theatre of his talents, it falls very short of
"the affection and reverence which I feel when I contem-
"plate the nobler parts of his character, in the sanctuary
"of his virtues. Of him I have said in a Dedication what
"to the latest hour of my life I will repeat and avow, and
"what I am prepared to defend amidst the dissolution of
"public parties, the mutations of public opinion, and the
"shocks of public events," p. 9. In this passage are crowded together all the faults of Johnson,—pomposity, affectation, and formality, inversion of the language, poverty and repetition of ideas. "I pronounce him an atrocious
"slanderer who could torture my undisguised scruples as to
"the irresistible necessity of an Antigallican war into the
"slightest

" flightest propensity to Gallican theories, Gallican extra-
" vagancies, or Gallican enormities," Ditto, p. 65, which
being translated into plain English, means, that it was unjust for any man to infer, from his aversion to the war, that
he was a friend to the enormities of the French. " To
" treasure up a copious store of specific and energetic appel-
" lations for public crimes, be their motives ever so flagi-
" tious, their aggravations ever so heinous, and their conse-
" quences ever so baleful," Ditto, p. 65. " The pur-
" chasers of fine books are not always readers of learned
" books, and the readers of learned books, who may them-
" selves stand least in need of being informed, are most ri-
" gorous in their requisitions for information to be given
" upon the sources from which notes are selected," p. 69.
This is formal and perplexed. The Doctor's controversial
works abound certainly with many fine passages, but in general the stile is heavy and pompous.

P. 44. The present state of this country, with regard
to the article of provisions, furnishes an additional argument in favour of what has been advanced on the danger of
trusting to speculative opinions, without sufficient experience;
and recent events have completely overturned the fine-
wrought and plausible theories of Dr Adam Smith and his
admirers; for the alarm of last year's scarcity having given
an opportunity to speculators in provisions to monopolize,
has so advanced them in price, that the lower classes of society are hardly able, by the severest industry, to earn a bare
subsistence: this monopoly being once established, it is extremely difficult to reduce things to their own proper level,
because it is supported by a paper credit, extended beyond
all the limits of convenience. And who is the better for all

this

this oppression and iniquity? not those who thus unjustly starve and torment their fellow-creatures; for their ill-gotten wealth can give them little enjoyment, and no one ultimately receives any advantage, but the revenue for the money which is extorted from the industrious poor by monopolizers and forestallers, is spent on the luxuries of life, all of which are severely taxed, while articles of the first necessity, the immediate produce of the land, which are the principal food of the poor, are not subject to taxation, so that the poor may be justly said to labor not for themselves but for others; this is an evil which will work its own cure by violent means, if not speedily redressed by such as are gentle. Without the interference of Government there is nothing left for those consumers, in the superior classes, who feel they are oppressed, but to agree with each other not to make use of those articles which are unjustly advanced, till they are considerably reduced in price. Let them be unanimous, and proceed with one thing after another, and they will attain their purpose.—" When bad men conspire, honest men " must unite;" they have no other remedy.

P. 68. Though it is sometimes difficult to settle, with accuracy, the chronology of the works of our antient poets, yet it is neither a fruitless nor a useless search, as it marks the first dawnings and progress of genius, by enabling us to prove the variations of their different editions. The neglect of this accuracy is very frequent in the biographers of our numerous poets; but in none more than in the late R. Walpole, for, in his Life of Lord Buckhurst, he speaks of the Mirror, as being first published in 1610. For more accurate information I refer my reader to the *Theatrum Poetarum Anglicanorum*, lately re-published.

P. 69.

P. 69. The defects of this book are so numerous, that I have not room here to point them out; in one subject alone it will be sufficient, and this may leave my readers to imagine the same in others. The department of poetry I will take as an instance; and what ought we to think of a Professor who writes on the subject of Belles Lettres, and omits to criticise many species of poetry, and some of our best Poets?—His general remarks on pastoral poetry are in many places borrowed, word for word, from Johnson's Rambler, N° 36; and, in others, "disfigured, as gypsies "do stolen children, to prevent their being found out." To what are we to attribute his having never once mentioned the Pastorals of Spenser, and the Arcadia of Sir P. Sidney. The latter, though not written in verse, is highly poetical in its language and characters; but this cannot be objected as his excuse, because he has noticed Telemachus. The Pastoral Poems of Spenser deserve rather to be noticed for their faults than their beauties, for their coarse language and unnatural allegory. The remarks on lyric poetry are equally defective; two lines are all he bestows on Gray, and Akenside is never mentioned; nor the choruses in Mason's tragedies. The praises of J. B. Rousseau, which have been echoed from one French critic to another, and repeated injudiciously by Warton, are here repeated again; but let it be remembered, that morality in verse is not poetry, yet his Cantatas, which are never noticed, are the most truly poetical of all his numerous works, the most of which are below mediocrity. His enumeration of epic poems contains two pieces of Ossian, which owe their place there entirely to national prejudice. The epithet beautiful, in his remarks on tragedy, seems ill applied to the most terrific choruses of Æschylus; and he certainly is mistaken in saying

ing that the tragedies of Racine contain more incidents, more paſſion, and more buſtle, than thoſe of the Greeks, which were his model. One ſpecies of poetry he has entirely omitted. The Mock Heroic, or burleſque; ſuch are Garth's Diſpenſary, Phillips's Splendid Shilling, the Dunciad, the Lutrin, the Rape of the Lock, the Fribbeleriad of Garrick, and the Secchia Rapita, by Taſſoni: under this title is included the Macaronic poem, a ſpecies of humor of which we have but few ſpecimens; one by Drummond, is the beſt of the ſort before the time of the author, and another, publiſhed within theſe few years, attributed to Dr Geddes, and now out of print. But, of all his omiſſions, the moſt culpable is that of the Sonnet, a ſpecies of poetry unknown to the Greek and Latin writers, and in which ours have excelled their models. The Elegy is another ſpecies of poetry which Dr Blair has entirely omitted to notice; a tender, plaintive ſtrain, adapted to pour forth the gentle emotions of ſorrow, and not unfrequently to vent the complaints of love. Tibullus, among the antients, and Hammond, among our own writers, are thoſe who have principally excelled.

P. 89. The Treatiſes, here mentioned, I found by accident in the rare and curious library of Emanuel College, a copious repoſitory of human wiſdom and human folly; where I have diſturbed the duſt of many a neglected author, for alternate wearineſs and delight. The ingenious and induſtrious Robert Robinſon, in his ſpirited but ill-written Eccleſiaſtical Reſearches, has noticed this fiery inquiſitor, and given a ſhort account of his character, views, and ſentiments.

ADDITIONS.

TO the Sonnets which are here subjoined, as specimens of the different writers in that species of poetry, I have ventured to add two, which, I believe, are now out of print; the one I met with in an old Magazine, the other is by a person whom I once had the happiness to call my friend: they are both of singular merit, and deserve to be reprinted.

SONNETS.

BY THE EARL OF SURREY.

Ed. CURLL, 1717.

Request to his Love to joyne Bounty with Beautye.

THE golden Gift that Nature did thee geve,
To fasten Frendes, and feede them at thy wyll
With Fourme and Favour, taught me to beleve,
How thou art made to shewe her greatest skill.
Whose hydden Vertues are not so unknowen,
But lively Dames might gather at the first,
Where Beautye so her perfect Seede hath sowen,
Al other Graces followe nedes there must.
Now certesse Ladye, since al this is true,
That from above thy Giftes are thus elect,
Doe not deface them then with Fansies newe.
Nor chaunge of Mindes let not the Mynde infecte,

But Mercy him thy Frende, that doth thee ferve,
Who fekes alway thine Honour to preferve.

To fhew how the poets of former times bedaubed each other with praifes, I have given two complimentary ftrains from Spenfer and Raleigh, which hardly deferve the title with which they are honored, for a fonnet ought not to convey a compliment but a complaint.

To the right noble and valorous Knight, Sir Walter Raleigh, Lord Wardein of the Stanneryes, and Lieftenaunt of Cornewail.

To thee, that art the fommer's nightingale,
Thy fovereign goddeffes moft dear delight,
Why do I fend this ruftic madrigale,
That may thy tunefull ear unfeafon quite?
Thou onely fit this argument to write,
In whofe high thoughts pleafure hath beult her boure,
And dainty love learned fweetly to endite,
My rimes, I know, unfavoury and foure:
To tafte the ftreams that, like a golden fhoure,
Flow from thy fruitful hede, of thy love's praife,
When fo thee lift thy lofty Mufe to raife;
Yet till that thou thy poeme wilt make knowne,
Let thy fair Cynthia's praifes be thus rudely fhowne.

A Vifion upon the Conceipt of the Faery Queene.

METHOUGHT I faw the grave where Laura lay,
Within that temple where the veftall flame

Was wont to burne, and paffing by that way,
To fee that buried duft of living fame,
Whofe tumb fair love and fairer virtue kept,
All fuddeinly I faw the faery Queene,
At whofe approache the foul of Petrarke wept;
And from thenceforth thofe Graces were not feene,
For they this Queene attended, in whofe ftead
Oblivion laid him down upon Laura's herfe,
Hereat the hardeft ftones were feen to bleed,
And grones of buried ghoftes the heaven did perfe;
Where Homer's fprite did tremble all for griefe,
And curft the accefs of that celeftial thiefe.

DRAYTON.

Ed. 1753, p. 1260.

Bright ftar of beauty, on whofe eye-lids fit
A thoufand nymph-like and enamour'd graces,
The goddeffes of memory and wit,
Which there in order take their feveral places,
In whofe dear bofom fweet delicious Love
Lays down his quiver which he once did bear,
Since he that bleffed paradife did prove,
And leaves his mother's lap to fport him there;
Let others ftrive to entertain with words,
My foul is of a braver metal made,
I hold that vile, which vulgar wit affords;
In me's that faith which time cannot invade.
 Let what I praife be ftill made good by you:
 Be you moft worthy, whilft I am moft true.

DRUMMOND.

Dear chorister, who from those shadows sends,
Ere that the blushing morn dare shew her light,
Such sad lamenting strains, that night attends
(Become all ear), stars stay to hear thy plight;
If one whose grief even reach of thought transcends,
Who ne'er (not in a dream) did taste delight,
May thee importune who like case pretends,
And seems to joy in woe, in woe's despite;
Tell me (so may thou fortune milder try,
And long long sing!) for what thou thus complains,
Since winter's gone, and sun in dappled sky
Enamour'd smiles on woods and flow'ry plains?
    The bird, as if my questions did her move,
    With trembling wings sigh'd forth, I love, I love.

DRUMMOND.

Sweet bird, that sing'st away the early hours
Of winters past, or coming, void of care,
Well pleased with delights which present are,
Fair seasons, budding sprays, sweet-smelling flow'rs:
To rocks, to springs, to rills, from leavy bow'rs
Thou thy Creator's goodness dost declare,
And what dear gifts on thee he did not spare,
A stain to human sense in sin that low'rs.
What soul can be so sick, which by thy songs
(Attir'd in sweetness) sweetly is not driven
Quite to forget earth's turmoils, spites, and wrongs,
And lift a reverend eye and thought to heaven?
    Sweet, artless songster, thou my mind dost raise
    To airs of spheres, yes, and to angels' lays.

DRUMMOND.

DRUMMOND.

Let us each day inure ourselves to die,
If this, and not our fears, be truly death,
Above the circles both of hope and faith
With fair immortal pinions to fly;
If this be death, our best part to untie,
By ruining the gaol, from lust and wrath,
And every drowsy langour here beneath,
To be made deniz'd citizen of sky;
To have more knowledge than all books contain,
All pleasures even surmounting wishing pow'r,
The fellowship of God's immortal train,
And these that time nor force shall e'er devour:
 If this be death, what joy, what golden care
 Of life, can with death's uglines compare?

To a Robin Red-Breast.

Dear, social bird, that oft, with fearless love,
 Giv'st thy soft form to man's protective care,
Pleas'd, when rude tempests vex the ruffled air,
For the warm roof, to leave the naked grove.

Kindest and last of summer's tuneful train,
 Ah! do not yet give o'er the plaintive lay,
 But charm mild Zephyr to a longer stay,
And oft renew thy sweetly-parting strain.

So when rough winter frowns with brow severe,
And chilling blasts shall strip the sheltering trees;
 When meagre want thy shivering frame shall seize,
And death, with dart uplifted, hover near;
 My grateful hand the liberal crumbs shall give,
 My bosom warm thee, and my kiss revive.

To the River Cam.

Whilst on thy sedgy banks I pensive stray,
And mark thy ling'ring waters silent lave
Thy rows of antient willows, as they wave
Their thin, pale foliage o'er thy level way,
Sternly does memory point the distant hour
Which to thy favored seats, too rashly gave
My untried youth, unskilled the spell to brave,
Of sloth's insidious smile, or pleasure's dulcet lay.
Sleep on, dull stream, emblem methinks of those
Thy pampered sons, who emulous no more,
The page of science as they rudely close,
Listless and sad, drag out the lengthened hour,
Or if more social mirth forbid repose,
With jests obscene, profane the muse's bower.

Though I have asserted, in p. 62, that the French have no writers of Sonnets, yet certainly they have some who have written poems under that name, yet whether they deserve it or no, my readers will judge when they see one that is reckoned among their finest, it is by Henault, a poet in the time of Louis XIV; the subject is rather unfavorable to poetical, or even moral delicacy, and the whole is nothing but point and overstrained antithesis; it is entitled the Abortion.

Toi qui meurs avant que de naitre,
Assemblage confus de l' être et du neant,
Triste Avorton, informe enfant,
Rebut du neant et de l' être !

Toi que l'amour fit par un crime,
Et que l'amour defait par un crime a son tour,
Funeste ouvrage de l'amour,
De l'honneur funeste victime,
Donne fin aux remords par qui tu t'es vengé,
Et du fond du neant oú je t'ai replongé
N'entretiens point l'horreur dont ma faute est suivie,
Deux tyrans opposés ont decidé ton sort ;
L'amour malgré l'honneur t'a fait donner la vie :
L'honneur malgré l'amour te fait donner la mort.

M. Sackuil's Induction.

The wrathfull winter proching on apace,
With blustering blasts had all ybarde the treene,
And olde Saturnus with his frosty face
With chilling cold had pearst the tender greene :
The mantles rent, wherein enwrapped beene
The gladsome groues that now lay ouerthrowne,
The tapets torne, and euery tree downe blowne.

The soyle that erst so seemly was to seene,
Was all despoyled of her beauties hewe :
And soote fresh flowers (wherewith the sommers Queene
Had clad the earth) now Boreas blasts downe blewe.
And small foules flocking, in theyr song did rewe
The winters wrath, wherewith ech thing defaste,
In woefull wise he wayld the sommer past.

Hawthorne had lost his motley liuery,
The naked twiges were shiuering all for cold :
And dropping downe the teares aboundantly,
Ech thing (mee thought) with weeping eye mee tolde
The cruell season, bidding mee withholde

My selfe within, for I was gotten out
Into the fieldes, whereas I walkt about.

And sorrowing I to see the sommer flowers,
The liuely greene, the lusty leafe forlorne,
The sturdy trees so shattred with the showers,
The fielde fade that florisht so beforne,
It taught me well all earthly things be borne
To dye the death, for nought long time may last.
The sommers beauty yeeldes to winters blast.

Then looking upward to the heauens leames
With nightes starres thicke powdred euery where,
Which erst so glistned with the golden streames
That chearfull Phœbus spred down from his sphere,
Beholding darke oppressing day so neare.
The sodayne sight reduced to my mynde,
The sundry chaunges that in earth wee finde.

That musing on this worldly wealth in thought,
Which comes and goes more faster than wee see
The flickring flame that with the fyre is wrought,
My bussie mynde presented unto mee
Such fall of Peeres as in the realme had bee:
That oft I wisht some would their woes descryue,
To warne the rest whome Fortune left a liue.

And strait forth stalking with redoubled pace,
For that I sawe the night drew on so fast,
In blacke all clad there fell before my face
A piteous wight, whom woe had all forewast,
Forth on her eyes the cristall tears out brast,
And sighing sore her hands she wrong and folde,
Tare all her hayre that ruth was to beholde.

Her

Her body smale forwithred and forspent,
As is the stalke that sommers drought oppreſt,
Her wealked face with woefull tears bee sprent,
Her colour pale, (as it seemed her best)
In woe and plaint repoſed was her rest.
And as the stone that drops of water weares,
So dented were her chekes with fall of teares.

Her eyes swollen with flowing streams aflote,
Where with her lookes throwne vp full piteously,
Her forceleſſe hands together oft shee smote,
With dolefull shrikes, that eckoed in the skye:
Whoſe plaint such sighes did strait accompany,
That in my doome was neuer man did see
A wight but halfe so woe begone as shee.

I stoode agaſt, beholding all her plight,
Tweene dread and dolour so diſtreinde in hart
That while my hayres upſtarted with the sight,
The tears out streamde for sorow of her smart:
But when I sawe no end that could appert
The deadly dewle, which she soe sore did make,
With dolefull voice then thus to her I spake:

Unwrap thy woes what euer wight thou bee,
And stint in tyme to spill thy self with playnt,
Tell what thou art, and whence, for well I see
Thou canſt not dure with sorrow thus attaynt.
And with that word of sorrow all forfaynt
Shee looked up, and proſtrate as shee lay
With piteous sound lo thus shee gan to say.

Alas, I wretch whom thus thou seest distraynde
With wasting woes that neuer shall aslake,
Sorrow I am, in endlesse torments paynde,
Among the Furies, in th' infernall lake,
Where Pluto God of Hell so griesly blacke
Doth holde his throne, and Lætheus deadly tast
Doth rieue remembraunce of ech thing forepast:

Whence come I am, the drery desteny
And lucklesse lot for to bemone of those,
Whome Fortune in this maze of misery,
Of wretched chaunce, most wofull Miroirs chose,
That when thou seest how lightly they did lose
Their pompe, their power, & that they thought most sure,
Thou mayst soone deeme no earthly ioy may dure.

Whose rufull voice no sooner had out brayed
Those wofull words, wherewith shee sorrowed so,
But out alas shee shright and neuer stayed,
Fell downe, and all to dasht her selfe for wo.
The cold pale dread my limmes gan ouergo,
And I so sorrowed at her sorrowes eft,
That what with griefe and feare my wits were reft.

I stretcht my selfe, and strait my hart reuiues,
That dread and dolour erst did so appale,
Like him that with the feruent feuer striues
When sicknesse seekes his calstell health to skale:
With gathred sprites so forst I feare to auale.
And rearing her with anguish all foredone,
My sprites return'd, and then I thus begon.

O Sorrow,

O Sorrow, alas sith Sorrow is thy name,
And that to thee this drere doth well pertayne,
In vayne it were to seeke to ceafe the fame:
But as a man himfelfe with forrow flayne,
So I alas doe comfort thee in payne,
That here in forrow art forfunke fo deepe,
That at thy fight I can but figh and weepe.

I had no fooner fpoken of a ftike
But that the ftorme fo rumbled in her breft,
As Eolus could neuer roare the like,
And fhowers downe raynde from her eyes fo faft,
That all bedreint the place, till at the laft
Well eafed they the dolour of her minde,
As drops of rayne doth fwage the ftormy winde.

For forth fhee paced in her fearefull tale:
Come, come (quod fhee) and fee what I fhall fhowe,
Come here the playning, and the bitter bale
Of worthy men, by Fortunes ouerthrowe.
Come thou and fee them rewing all in rowe.
They were but fhades that erft in minde thou rolde.
Come, come with mee, thine eyes fhall them beholde.

What coulde thefe wordes but make mee more agaft,
To heare her tell whereon I mufde while ere:
So was I mazde therewith: till at the laft,
Mufing upon her words, and what they were,
All fodaynly well leffoned was my feare:
For to my minde retourned how fhee teld
Both what fhee was, and where her wun fhee helde.

Whereby I knewe that fhe a Goddeffe was,
And therewithall reforted to my minde
My thought, that late prefented mee the glas
Of brittle ftate, of cares that here wee finde,
Of thoufand woes to feely men affynde:
And how fhee now bid me come and beholde
To fee with eye that earft in thought I rolde.

Flat downe I fell, and with all reuerence
Adored her, perceiuing now that fhee
A Goddeffe fent by godly prouidence,
In earthly fhape thus fhews her felfe to mee,
To wayle and rue this worlds uncertainty:
And while I honourd thus her Godheads might,
With plaining voyce thefe words fhee fhright.

I fhall thee guyde firft to the griefly lake,
And thence vnto the blifsfull place of reft,
Where thou fhalt fee and heare the playnt they make,
That whilome here bare fwinge among the beft.
This fhalt thou fee, but greate is the vnreft
That thou muft byde, before thou canft attayne
Unto the dreadfull place where thefe remayne.

And with thefe words as I vprayfed ftood,
And gan to followe her that ftraight forth pafte,
Ere I was ware, into a defert woode
We now were come: where hand in hand imbrafte
Shee led the way, and through the thicke fo trafte,
As but I had bene guided by her might,
It was no way for any mortall wight.

But

But loe, while thus amid the desert darke,
Wee passed on with steps and pace vnmeete,
A rumbling roare confusde with howle and barke
Of Dogs, shoke all the ground vnder our feete,
And stroke the din within our eares so deepe,
As halfe distraught vnto the ground I fell,
Besought retourne, and not to visite Hell.

But shee forthwith vplifting mee a pace
Remoude my dread, and with a stedfast minde
Bad mee come on, for here was now the place,
The place where wee our trauails end should finde.
Wherewith I rose, and to the place assignde
Astomde I stalkt, when strayght wee aproached nere
The dreadfull place, that you will dread to here,

And hideous hole all vaste, withouten shape,
Of endles depth, orewhelmde with ragged stone,
With ougly mouth, and griesly iawes doth gape,
And to our sight confounds it selfe in one.
Here entred wee, and yeeding forth, anone
An horrible lothly lake wee might discerne
As blacke as pitch, that cleped is Auerne.

A deadly gulfe where nought but rubbish grows,
With fowle blacke swelth in thickned lumps that lies,
Which vp in th' ayre such stinking vapors throws
That ouer there, may flie no fowle but dyes,
Choakt with the pestlent sauours that arise.
Hither wee come, whence forth wee still did pace,
In dreadfull feare amid the dreadfull place:

And

And first within the porch and iawes of Hell
Sate deepe Remorse of conscience, all bee sprent
With teares: and to her selfe oft would shee tell
Her wretchednes, and cursing neuer stent
To sob and sighe: but euer thus lament,
With thoughtfull care, as shee that all in vaine
Would were and waste continually in payne.

Her eyes vnstedfast rolling here and there,
Whurld on each place, as place that vengeaunce brought,
So was her minde continually in feare,
Tossed and tormented with tedious thought
Of those detested crymes which shee had wrought:
With dreadfull cheare and lookes throwne to the skie,
Wishing for death, and yet shee could not die.

Next sawe wee Dread all trembling how hee shooke,
With foote vncertayne profered here and there.
Benomd of speach, and with a ghastly looke
Searcht euery place all pale and dead for feare,
His cap borne vp with staring of his heare,
Stoynde and amazde at his owne shade for dreede,
And fearing greater daungers then was neede.

And next within the entry of this lake
Sate fell Reuenge gnashing her teeth for ire,
Deuising meanes how shee may vengeaunce take,
Neuer in rest till shee haue her desire:
But frets within so farforth with the fire
Of wreaking flames, that now determines shee
To dy by death, or vengde by death to bee.

When

When fell Reuenge with bloudy foule pretence
Had showde her selfe as next in order set,
With trembling lims wee softly parted thence,
Till in our eyes another sight wee met:
When fro my heart a sigh forthwith I fet,
Rewing alas vpon the woefull plight
Of Misery, that next appeard in sight.

His face was leane, and somedeale pynde away,
And eke his hands consumed to the bone,
But what his body was I cannot say,
For on his carkas rayment had hee none
Saue clouts and patches pieced one by one,
With staffe in hand, and scrip on shoulder cast,
His chiefe defence agaynst the winters blast.

His foode for most, was wilde fruites of the tree,
Vnlesse sometime some crums fell to his share,
Which in his wallet long God wot kept hee,
As one the which full daintely would fare.
His drinke the running streame: his cup the bare
Of his palme cloasde, his bed the hard cold ground
To this poore life was Misery ybound.

Whose wretched state when wee had well beheld,
With tender ruth on him and on his feres,
In thoughtfull cares, forth then our pace wee held.
And by and by, another shape apperes
Of greedy Care, still brushing vp the breres,
His knuckles knobde, his flesh deepe dented in,
With tawed hands, and hard ytanned skin.

The

The morrowe gray no sooner hath begon
To spreade his light euen peping in our eyes,
When hee is vp and to his work yrun.
But let the nights blacke misty mantles rise,
And with foule darke neuer so mutch disguise
The fayre bright day, yet ceasseth hee no while,
But hath his candels to prolong his toyle.

By him lay heauy Sleepe the cosin of Death
Flat on the ground, and still as any stone,
A very corps, saue yelding forth a breath.
Smale kepe tooke hee whome Fortune frowned on,
Or whom shee lifted vp into the throne
Of high renoune, but as a liuing death,
So dead aliue, of life hee drew the breath.

The bodies rest, the quiet of the hart,
The trauailes ease, the still nights feere was hee.
And of our life in earth the better part,
Reuer of sight, and yet in whom wee see
Things oft that tyde, and oft that neuer bee.
Without respect esteming equally
King Cræsus pompe, and Irus pouertie.

And next in order sad Old Age wee found,
His beard all hoare, his eyes hollow and blind,
With drouping chere still poring on the ground,
As on the place where nature him assinde
To rest, when that the sisters had vntwynde
His vitall thred, and ended with their knyfe
The fleting course of fast declyning lyfe.

There

There heard wee him with broke and hollow plaint
Rewe with him selfe his end approching fast,
And all for nought his wretched mind torment,
With sweete remembraunce of his pleasures past,
And fresh delytes of lusty youth forewast.
Recounting which, how would hee sob and shrike:
And to bee yong agayne of Ioue beseke.

But and the cruell fates so fixed bee,
That tyme forepast cannot retourne agayne,
This one request of Ioue yet prayed hee:
That in such withred plight, and wretched paine,
As eld (accompanied with his lothsome trayne)
Had brought on him, all were it woe and griefe,
Hee might a while yet linger forth his liefe,

And not so soone discend into the pit:
Where Death, when hee the mortall corps hath slayne,
With retchlesse hand in graue doth couer it,
Therafter neuer to enioy agayne
The gladsome light, but in the ground ylayne,
In depth of darknesse wast and weare to nought,
As hee had nere into the world bene brought.

But who had seene him, sobbing how hee stoode
Unto himselfe, and how hee would bemone
His youth forepast, as though it wrought him good
To talke of youth, all were his youth foregone,
Hee would haue musde and meruaylde much whereon
This wretched Age should life desire so fayne,
And knowes full well lyfe doth but length his payne.

T   Crookebackt

Crookebackt hee was, toothshaken, and blere eyde,
Went on three feete and somtyme crept on fowre,
With olde lame boanes, that ratled by his syde,
His scalpe all pild, and hee with eld forlore:
His withred fist still knocking at Deaths dore,
Fumbling and driueling as hee drawes his breath,
For briefe, the shape and messenger of Death.

And fast by him pale Malady was plaste,
Sore sicke in bed, her colour all foregone,
Bereft of stomacke, sauour, and of taste,
Ne could shee brooke no meate but broths alone.
Her breath corrupt, her kepers euery one
Abhorring her, her sicknes past recure,
Detesting phisicke, and all phisickes cure.

But oh the dolefull sight that then wee see,
Wee tournd our looke, and on the other side
A griesly shape of Famine mought wee see,
With greedy lookes, and gaping mouth that cryed,
And roarde for meate as shee should there haue dyed,
Her body thin, and bare as any bone,
Whereto was left nought but the case alone.

And that alas was gnawne on euery where,
All full of holes, that I ne mought refrayne
From tears, to see how shee her armes could teare,
And with her teeth gnash on the bones in vayne:
When all for nought shee fayne would so sustayne
Her starued corps, that rather seemde a shade,
Then any substaunce of a creature made.

Great was her force, whome stone wall could not stay,
Her tearing nayles snatching at all shee saw:
With gaping iawes, that by no meanes ymay
Be satisfide from hunger of her mawe,
But eates herselfe as shee that hath no lawe:
Gnawing, alas, her carkas all in vayne,
Where you may count ech sinew, bone, and vayne.

On her while wee thus firmly fixt our eyes,
That bled for ruth of such a drery sight,
Loe sodaynly shee shrikt in so huge wise,
As made Hell gates to shiuer with the might.
Wherewith a dart wee sawe how it did light
Right on her brest, and therewithall pale Death
Enthrilling it to reue her of her breath.

And by and by a dum dead corps wee sawe,
Heauy and colde, the shape of death aright,
That daunts all earthly creatures to his lawe:
Against whose force in vaine it is to fight.
Ne Peeres, ne Princes, nor no mortall wyght,
No Townes, ne Realmes, Cittyes, ne strongest Tower,
But all perforce must yeelde vnto his power.

His dart anon out of the corps hee tooke,
And in his hand (a dreadfull sight to see)
With great tryumph eftsones the same hee shooke,
That most of all my feares affrayed mee.
His body dight with nought but bones perdye,
The naked shape of man there saw I plaine,
All saue the flesh, the sinow, and the vaine.

Lastly stoode Warre in glittering armes yclad,
With visage grym, sterne lookes, and blackly hewed,
In his right hand a naked sworde hee had,
That to the hilts was all with bloud embruyed:
And in his left (that King and kingdomes rewed)
Famine and fyer he held, and therewithall
He razed townes, and threw downe towres and all.

Cities he sakt, and realmes that whileome flowred
In honour, glory, and rule aboue the best
Hee ouerwhelmde, and all theire fame deuoured,
Consumde, destroyde, wasted and neuer ceast,
Tyll hee theire wealth, theire name and all oppreft,
His face forehewde with wounds, and by his side
There hung his targ, with gashes deepe and wide.

In mids of which, depainted there wee founde
Deadly Debate, all full of snaky heare,
That with a bloudy fillet was ybound,
Out beeathing nought but discord euery where.
And round about were portrayde here and there
The hugy hostes, Darius and his power,
His Kings, Princes, his Peeres, and all his flower.

Here from when scarce I could mine eyes withdrawe
That fylde with tears as doth the springing Well,
Wee passed on so far forth till we sawe
Rude Acheron, a lothsome lake to tell,
That boyles and bubs vp swelth as blacke as hell,
Where griesly Charon at theyr fixed tyde
Still ferries ghostes vnto the farder side.

The

The aged God no sooner Sorrow spyed,
But hasting straight vnto the bancke apace,
With hollowe call vnto the rout hee cryed,
To swarue apart, and gieue the Goddesse place.
Strayt it was done, when to the shore wee pace,
Where hand in hand as wee than linked fast,
Within the boate wee are together plaste,

And forth wee launch full fraughted to the brinke,
Whan with th' vnwonted waight, the rusty keele
Began to cracke as if the same should sinke.
Wee hoyse vp maste and sayle, that in a while
Wee fet the shoare, where scarsely wee had while
For to ariue, but that wee heard anone
A three sound barke confounded all in one.

Wee had not long forth past, but that wee sawe
Black Cerberus the hydeous hound of hell,
With bristles reard, and with a three mouth'd Iawe,
Foredinning th' ayre with his horrible yell.
Out of the deepe darke caue where hee did dwell,
The Goddesse straight hee knewe, and by and by
He peast and couched, while that wee past by.

Thence come wee to the horrour and the hell,
The large great Kingdoms, and the dreadfull raigne
Of Pluto in his throne where hee did dwell,
The wide waste places, and the hugie playne:
The waylings, shrikes, and sondry sorts of payne,
The sighes, the sobs, the deepe and deadly groane,
Earth, ayre, and all resounding playnt and moane.

Heare

Heare pewled the babes, and here the maydes vnwed,
With folded hands theyr sory chaunce bewayld:
Here wept the guiltles slayne, and louers dead,
That slew them selues when nothing els auayld:
A thousand sorts of sorrowes here that waylde
With sighs and teares, sobs, shrikes, and all yfeare,
That (oh alas) it was a hell to heare.

Wee staide vs strait, and with a rufull feare,
Beheld this heauy sight, while from myne eyes,
The vapored tears downe stilled here and there,
And Sorrowe eke in far more wofull wise,
Tooke on with plaint, vp heauing to the skies
Her wretched hands, that with her cry the rout
Gan all in heapes to swarme vs round about.

Loe here (quoth Sorrow) Princes of renoune,
That whilom sate on top of Fortunes wheele,
Now layde full low, like wretches whurled downe,
Euen with one frowne, that stayde but with a smyle.
And now beholde the thing that thou erewhile
Saw onely in thought, and what thou now shalt heere
Recompt the same to Kesar, King, and Peere.

Then first came Henry Duke of Buckingham,
His cloake of blacke alt pilde and quite forworne,
Wringing his hands, and Fortune oft doth blame,
Which of a Duke hath made him now her skorne.
With gastly lookes as one in maner lorne,
Oft spred his armes, stretcht hands hee ioynes as fast,
With rufull cheare, and vapored eyes vpcast.

His

His cloake hee rent, his manly breſt hee beat,
His hayre all torne about the place it lay,
My heart ſo molt to ſee his griefe ſo great,
As felingly me thought it dropt away:
His eyes they whurld about withouten ſtay,
With ſtormy ſighes the place did ſo complayne,
As if his heart at ech had burſt in twayne.

Thriſe hee began to tell his dolefull tale,
And thriſe the ſighes did ſwallow vp his voyce,
At ech of which he ſhriked ſo withall,
As though the heauens riued with the noyſe:
Till at the laſt recouering his voyce.
Supping the teares that all his breſt beraynde,
On cruell Fortune weeping thus he playnde.

Ed. Marſh, 1587.

The following Thoughts appeared, at different Times, in the Cambridge Intelligencer.

FRENCH GOVERNMENT.

To the EDITOR *of the* CAMBRIDGE INTELLIGENCER.

SIR,

THE probability of peace being now supposed to rest solely on the stability of the new French government; it is a matter of the utmost importance, to enquire how that is to be proved. Those who are desirous to defer the period of peace, will insist on time as the only criterion, while others who look for the future stability of governments, not in their past duration only, but in their merits, will readily acknowledge that the continuance of the new French constitution depends on its own character, and that of those by whom it is administered.—Should we be condemned to trust to time alone, for the prospect of peace, I fear the happy event is yet far distant, for time is an indefinite term, and our ministers are unwilling to define it: time is their safest refuge, their never-failing resource; time however may swallow up the present generation, before their hopes are realized, and entail the curses of war on our posterity; " It requires at least fifty years," says one of the friends of ministry, " for any new power " or constitution to find its level."* If this be true, our state is hopeless indeed: yet time, though it may strengthen a government, does not always improve it: and if it be objected, to the present government of France that it is new, it might be easy to name many others on the Continent, which are not better because they are older. Time then is so far from being a criterion of the probable stability of a government, that the oldest are nearest their dissolution, at least those which are new, cannot be proved to be nearer. The want of age was never objected to the late constitution of France, why should it then to the present? the throne of Rewbell was not longer fixed, than that of Bonaparte,

* Pursuits of Literature, p. 169.

Bonaparte, yet our ministers did not hesitate to negociate with him. The probable stability of a government then is no more to be determined by time, than the life of a man by its past duration, rather than by his health. We will look then for the permanency of the French government in its own intrinsic merit, and the merits of those by whom it is administered. In a government where great power is given to one or more individuals, the character and effects of that government, will always depend much on the temper of its principal agents, independent of the principles upon which it is established: such is precisely the case in France. The government is founded on the principles of liberty and equality; yet so great is the power given to its first Consul, that the prosperity of the country, in a great measure, depends on the wisdom and vigor of his conduct; and hitherto we have seen nothing to make us doubt his success; for in spite of all the coarse illiberality with which he has been reviled, I will venture to maintain, that while his virtues and his talents are exerted as they have been, they must ultimately produce the good and happiness of his country; for it has been
his

his conſtant endeavour to reconcile all parties, to conciliate all his enemies, and to diſſolve all oppoſition by the gentle influence of moderation and mildneſs, by yielding to inveterate habits, by reſpecting ancient prejudices, and reconciling the oppoſite antipathies of different parties: it is here then we are to look for the ſtability of the new government, in the total difference of conduct which has marked every act of its adminiſtration, from all thoſe which preceded it, and in the ſatisfaction with which it has been received by the people; every hideous mark of revolution is effaced, and I defy any one to produce a ſingle inſtance of cruelty, injuſtice, or tyranny committed by the new rulers of France. The irritating petulance of manifeſtoes and public addreſſes is abandoned, and the firſt Conſul, truſting rather to deeds than to words for his credit, both at home and abroad, has been very ſparing in his proclamations and profeſſions; and on all the late tranſactions reſpecting peace, has preſerved a degree of ſilent dignity, which does honour to his magnanimity and prudence, *while he is preparing with zeal and activity to enſure thoſe fu-*

ture successes which will astonish all Europe, and avenge more completely than by words, the insults he has received from this country. I have here said all that I choose to say on the character of Bonaparte, or I might contrast him with the rulers of other nations. What I have said is sufficient to shew my opinion—he has regenerated France, and in a few years his character, combined with the principles of the French revolution, will have such an influence on the affairs of the world, as that of no other individual ever yet had in any age or country.

Morpeth, March 9.   W. B.

FRENCH GOVERNMENT.

To the EDITOR *of the* CAMBRIDGE INTELLIGENCER.

SIR,

WHILE men are debating about theories, they often lose sight of much practical good; the experience of ages ought to teach us not to expect too much from human nature, and in the progress of improvement to proceed by slow and gentle steps; it remains yet to be proved, whether men can ever be so pure and happy as some moralists have imagined; past experience pronounces the contrary, yet that is frequently contradicted by new occurrences. Guided by these principles, I will attempt to examine the present French Constitution, impartially, because it contradicts some of the sanguine expectations I had formed of the progress of Liberty; deliberately, because I have waited to see the opinions of others, and honestly, because I have no interest in its success, but in the general good it is likely to produce. The main object of all good government is to secure the people from the opposite evils of despotism, and anarchy; from the oppression of individuals, and the oppression of each other: two evils which naturally tend to their extremes; despotism produces anarchy, and anarchy begets despotism; this has been exemplified by the state of France, for these last ten years. Liberty, as far as it can be secured under any human institution, till mankind are more generally enlightened, exists in the medium between these

these two extremes: men are not yet pure enough to govern themselves, they must feel the force of law, and the power of authority. A government purely representative, or a government where representation is disregarded, must degenerate into tyranny; the great secret is, to make the government and the people reciprocally feel the force of each other: wisdom is the best qualification, though it does not form an exclusive right to govern, as some men have imagined, but wisdom is not always the lot of the people; let their choice then be corrected by those whom education has given greater ability to judge wisely.

The basis of the new French Constitution, is the right of the people to choose their own rulers; but it does not stop here, for this principle, though plausible in theory, has been found by experience to be attended with danger; it is modified and corrected by tempering strict right, with superior wisdom; the constitution has its root in the people, and its branches flourish only by their support; it acknowledges the controul of public opinion by being submitted to their acceptance, and so far from being a usurpation

tion of their rights, it delivered them from the hands of usurpers, and effectually secured them against future encroachment. Out of five thousand men chosen by the people, it will be hard if there cannot be found five hundred, possessing talents and integrity, to be selected by others, whom in the present instance it will not be denied are eminently qualified for the office; and these men, though they may not propagate wisdom, may at least judge of it in those who are offered to their choice, to recruit their own body in case of death: there is no danger that they should form a junto of their own friends, for they have not the nomination of the candidates, but the government and the councils have each their share. The principle of popular choice, so far from being abandoned in any part of the state, is made the first requisite for all popular administrations: they must be chosen out of a list formed by the people. In despotic monarchies every thing emanates from the Sovereign, all look up to him; here every thing emanates from the people, though it finds its completion in the government. The Conservate Senate is to be considered as the barrier

between

between arbitrary power, and democratic violence: they are the bottom on which the constitution is built, whether it is rock or sand, is hardly to be doubted: they cannot be openly corrupted, because they can accept of no place, they are made independent by their salaries, and the public purse is so well guarded as to deprive the Consul of all power to corrupt them in secret. This Senate is invested with a controuling power over the acts of the legislature, not generally nor arbitrarily, but only in certain cases referred to them by the Tribunate: their power of selecting the legislative bodies justly entitles them to the name of conservative; for on these depend the safety of the state, and without they are weak or corrupt, it can never be in danger. It is this part of the government which seems to take most from its democratic quality, but the experience of ten years has proved that some balance was requisite against the weakness of the people, to prevent their power from being made the engine of faction, or the sport of tyranny. The power of proposing laws, entrusted to the government, has given the greatest offence to the ardent

friends

friends of freedom; yet it is a power not wholly destructive of liberty, as we have seen in our own country, and if it tends in some measure to deprive them of the chance of being popular, it is corrected by another power, the power of rejecting them, which, if they remain uncorrupt, is a sufficient security for the rights of the people. Let it be remembered that I do not speak of a government positively free, but of such a medium between monarchy and entire liberty as the state of the country will permit:—a country just emerged from the corruption of despotism, and hardly purified from her former filth. Such a government as is formed on the knowledge of the state of the people for whom it is intended, and not for men in the utmost state of purity. A government considerably removed from despotism, yet not advanced to complete liberty. To say that it has no defects, is ridiculous, but they are such as could not have been avoided, considering the state of the times. Such is the government by which the French may be happy, if the restlessness of their nature will permit: such is the government which the violent, in both extremes, have united to reprobate, and leaped over the space between them, to join hands with each other. Such is the government which the temperate only will admire, and admire it the more because it is condemned by the violent of all parties. —The force of prejudice was perhaps never more fully displayed than in the means which have been employed to vilify this government, and its first minister; the Royalist, to condemn it, affects a regard for the rights of the people, and the Democrat has reviled it because it is not aristocratical. Peltier* and the Morning Post have met together,— Mallet du Pan † and the Morning Chronicle have kissed each other. Yet great must be the blindness or the prejudice of that man who can compare Bonaparte to Robespierre, or apply the same epithets to the one as to the other; that this should be done by the hirelings of power, is not to be wondered at, for Bonaparte is more formidable to them than the other. Yet that men who consider themselves the advocates of truth, should have dwelt, with malignant pleasure, on what they call an act of usurpation,

* Paris, Vol. 25.
† Mercure Britannique, N° 32.

pation, and studiously or hastily detract from every act of lenity or mercy exercised by the first Consul, is rather to be imputed to their zeal, than their wisdom or their temper. I will ask of these intemperate friends of liberty, in what he has offended?—He exerted with vigour and promptness the only means in his power to dispossess a set of tyrants, and * usurpers, and restored the people to the exercise of their rights, somewhat limited and modified—if they are not again violated, he deserves praise, for what he has done, rather than censure for what he could not do with prudence. Here then is the state in which the French are placed by their new Constitution. The rights of all are acknowledged and protected, though some are privileged above others, yet not by birth, but by office: all men are equally eligible to public employments, for which they are to be recommended by the people, though selected by the Senate or Consul.—The personal liberty of every individual is strictly secured, so that no man is subject to arbitrary

* Usurpers they were, who had annulled all popular elections contrary to their own interest.

arbitrary arrest, or tedious detention. There is no power in any part of the government to oppress the people, nor can they obstruct the government in the exercise of its constitutional functions. The first Consul is surrounded by a body of Counsellors, for every department of the state, not solely of his own choice, but out of a limited number presented by the people, for whose interest they are to frame, and to whose representatives they are to present laws, with the consent of the Consul; so that every law is to be the result of the joint will of the government, and the people, and has the advantage of being deliberated three separate times; the great controul of public opinion is established by the formation of national lists, which form a standing testimony to those enrolled on them, of the approbation of their fellow Citizens: that these elections cannot be bribed by the government is to be expected from the exposure of the public accounts: that they cannot be bribed by individuals is certain, because they are too numerous, and that they cannot be influenced by the hopes of preferment, is also certain, because the

elected

elected and not the electors are alone eligible to all public employments.

To the safeguard and vigilance of the people is this constitution entrusted; it establishes no arbitrary distinctions of birth, and riches, no dominion over the rights of conscience—no exclusive privileges destructive of the happiness of others; every man is left to the free exercise of his industry, the free enjoyment of his professions, the free and full expression of his sentiments. This is perhaps the last experiment, should it fail, that will ever be tried for the attainment of happiness on the principle of equal rights; should it succeed, these rights may hereafter be exercised with greater freedom. It is only by experiment, that wisdom is to be gained, and it is only by being too hasty in experiments, that our happiness is endangered. While difference of opinions prevails, (and who will say that it will ever cease) mankind will never be entirely peaceable, yet many important grounds of difference may yet be removed: the wisdom of the world has hitherto been so equally divided, as to keep it in perpetual disturbance: yet some men will

say

say that this agitation is indispensible, as in water to prevent it becoming stagnant: nevertheless they do their fellow creatures the greatest kindness who endeavour to instil into them the sentiments of peace and harmony. The character of Bonaparte has undoubtedly had great influence in the formation of the constitution; it partakes of that sound wisdom, for which he has ever been distinguished. He has redeemed a whole people from moral and political degradation, and improved the condition of his species—whether it will be in his power to procure for them speedily the blessings of peace, is yet doubtful, but at present he must prepare for war. When he has passed the time of probation required of him by the British ministry, and brought proofs of his good behaviour before the Cabinet Council, when he is strong enough to repel all attempts on France, to compel Germany to accept his offers, and to shew that he cannot be resisted, he may then be thought worthy to negociate on equal terms with the immaculate ministers of this country, and be permitted to purchase for the world, and for France, the blessings of peace and tranquillity. Such is he at present,

sent,—the friend of man, and of his country,—whether power will have its usual effect of corruption on him, time only can determine! W. B.

Morpeth, April 9.

PRINCIPLES.

BY what means a man may best promote the happiness of his species, and gratify a laudable ambition for distinction? is a question worthy an intelligent being; in the various departments of life, each man may be useful if he pleases, yet there are many who pass their time in no other pursuit than that of pleasure, and seeking how they may gratify themselves without any regard to the happiness of others; such a life cannot be blameless, for when we think of the sum of misery in the world, the unequal distribution of its comforts, and the means it contains of rendering all men happy, or at least comfortable, it is surely no innocent occupation to be employed solely in the thoughts of our own amusement: when we think how many might be made happy with
the

the surplus wealth of others, and how many perish for want, while others have more than they enjoy, it is surely well worth enquiry—why these things are so, and whether they might not be otherwise? It is undoubtedly true that the world has hitherto been governed, and will continue to be governed, by a few general maxims, and on the truth and utility of these maxims the happiness of mankind must depend; if these are erroneous, the consequence will be misery and vice; if they are true, the result must be virtue and happiness. It is by first principles alone, that all arts are regulated, and as the art of government is capable of being reduced to such principles, it is on the rectitude of these alone, that the happiness of society depends; if these are not true, society can never arrive at the excellence of which it is supposed to be capable. Hitherto men have not been actuated in the formation of governments by principle, but directed by chance and convenience; the best government that exists, has been formed by time and experiment, but from these experiments have been deduced certain principles, which ought henceforth to form the basis of all political

litical societies, and thus, by further experiment, we acquire new principles. A spirit of investigation has now gone forth, and is spreading in every direction over all the arts of life, and even over the great art on which all others depend, the art of government: it is not by crude maxims hastily formed, hastily adopted, and transmitted without examination from one age to another, that mankind will henceforth be governed; they will require the test of experience for all the maxims they adopt, and judge of the value of opinions, not by the authority of those from whom they come, but by their own judgment. Mankind have hitherto been deceived by the authority of names, and foolishly supposed that because a man is great in some things, he must be great in all, though nothing is more certain than the fallibility of human judgment, and the difficulty of discovering truth upon a slight examination; it is therefore of the utmost consequence in education, to teach young people the exercise of their own judgment on all occasions, whereas education has hitherto tended only to teach them to rely on the authority of others: there is no doubt that the faculty of judgment acquires strength like all our other faculties, by exercise; it is of infinite use, therefore, to habituate young people to use it on every thing which is to be the subject of belief or practice; it is of more consequence to know a little thoroughly, than to know a great deal superficially. To acquire knowledge is in the power of most people, but to know the grounds of knowledge requires examination and patience; one day spent in the acquisition of principles, is worth years passed in merely swallowing down facts and opinions, without method or judgment. A well-known superficial coxcomb, whose works have tended to sap the foundation of every thing sincere and solid, for ever stunned the ears of his son with *the graces, the graces, the graces:* but a father who wishes his child to be truly valuable and useful, should never cease to repeat to him— PRINCIPLES, PRINCIPLES, PRINCIPLES; for PRINCIPLES are every thing: once teach a young man to know the ground and foundation of every thing he learns, the first principles on which every thing depends, once teach him to act and to judge from principle, and you have fixed the conduct of his life

life in a sure and certain path: but at present the generality of men act only from the impulse of the moment, from sordid interest, or temporary convenience; hence it is that few men are at all times to be trusted; and it is impossible for a man to be regularly and constantly good, without he acts upon principle. By the unceasing researches of men qualified to examine and to judge, a body of principles is now forming which will direct the future conduct of the world, and fix every species of knowledge on a sure basis; by a multitude of experiments only can any principle be ascertained; it is the same in chemistry, in agriculture, and in morality; the actual existence of certain qualities, and the actual utility of certain maxims, must be proved before they can form a ground of knowledge or of conduct. Whatever, therefore, is capable of being proved by experiment is knowledge, whatever is not is mere opinion, and deserves to be regarded only as such: opinion leads to knowledge, but experiment is the end of the journey. Superior wisdom suggests the probability of certain facts or opinions being true, but patient experiment only can prove them to be so:

it is from neglecting the one, and resting too confidently in the other, that the world has hitherto been so frequently misled. While men are governed by opinions, they must be for ever liable to error, doubt, and uncertainty: they must be for ever at variance with each other, and unsettled in themselves. Whenever they are guided solely by that which their faculties enable them to prove and comprehend, doubt and uncertainty will vanish; and all disputes about the nature of matter and spirit, pre-existence and eternity, &c. with all the miseries and murders they have occasioned, will for ever cease. Men will seek to know only what may be known, and leave all questions relating to other essences, to those superior beings by whom alone they can be comprehended.

Morpeth, April 30th.   W. B.

TO the want of any principles, or the adoption of false ones, are to be attributed most of the miseries of the world:—it is a defect which can only be remedied early in life, and therefore much depends on the education

cation of youth.—For the truth of this position I will only refer to the world at large, but principally to the higher and lower ranks; the former are hardly ever taught any principle but that of honour, which is a false one; and the latter, have no means of learning any; their interest, mere temporary interest, is their first object, and if they learn to restrain their passions, it is not from any principle of rectitude, but from the fear of punishment, or the hope of immediate interest. Now, till the motives of human conduct are taught to flow from a purer source, it is needless to expect purity, regularity, and integrity, or a state of society, tranquil, peaceable, and refined by the feelings of mutual confidence. The only solid and permanent principle of conduct, is the conviction that by acting humanely and justly to others, we promote our own happiness. Without the constant operation of this general principle, there can be no such thing as general happiness, and with it we banish effectually general misery. Should it be thought that I have too partially excepted the middle ranks of society from this general censure, I will only say, that I do not mean to do so entirely;

ly; for though their education is not without principles, yet they are frequently erroneous, and seldom take sufficient root to bear the violence and deceitfulness of the world. The principle of honour, by which the conduct of the higher ranks is partly regulated, I have stated to be a false one, and it is false, because it rests solely on partial opinion, and not on general utility; it is an imaginary standard, formed only by the convention of a few individuals, and is frequently contrary to the principles of truth and justice; its maxims are arbitrary, fluctuating, and contradictory, and its effects are not virtue, and general happiness, but private convenience and general misery: honour commands an affront to be expiated by the risque of life, and sometimes by death: truth and justice require only an acknowledgment of the fault, and the condemnation of public opinion, and public reproof. Honour is satisfied, in many instances, with a partial application of justice, as in the payment of our debts, of which some only are denominated debts of honour; while others, contracted under the strictest obligations of justice, may be left unpaid without any loss of credit or character: honour

nour depends not on any fixed principle, for what is honourable one day, may be disgraceful the next: and the honour of a soldier consists in obeying the commands of a superior, of which he neither examines the justice nor propriety.

But honour is not the only principle which regulates the conduct of the higher ranks, for where interest is concerned, honour yields her place with little reluctance; neither has she power to controul the effect of the passions by any consideration of the evil they occasion; for it will be found, that the most unlimited gratification of the worst of our evil propensities, is thoroughly compatible with the principle of honour, which is not like justice, rigid, inflexible, and extensive.

Another principle among people in high life, equally erroneous, and equally destructive, is to follow implicitly the dictates of fashion and custom; to this every thing valuable is sacrificed; under the authority of fashion, society is no longer the intercourse of congenial souls, but a mere unconnected crowd, where pride, envy, malice, indifference, vanity, and deceit, are the constant vifitors, and where gambling supplies the place of worse employment; or it is the unavailing resource of languor and vacuity, the constant companions of a fashionable education; in the empire of fashion, the most amiable virtues are laughed out of countenance, and a spurious kind of charity, the child of ostentation, is the only one suffered to intrude: friendship is but a fine name for long acquaintance, and every thing else seems what it is not: comfort, convenience, and health, are sacrificed to appearance, and even dress is not an article of use, but of vanity; truth, openness, and sincerity of manners, are banished for their vulgarity; and simplicity, the child of nature, gives place to deception and artifice: in short, no man follows his own opinion, but the opinion of others, and each man is the slave of his neighbour, while he thinks he is pursuing his own inclinations; he neither does nor avoids any thing because it is right or wrong, but because it is fashionable or vulgar. Taste, opinion, and virtue, are thus sacrificed to a phantom, which is for ever taking different shapes, and for ever misleads men from nature, truth, and simplicity, from all that is virtuous, amiable, and right.

Such,

Such, with a few exceptions, is the picture of high life, under the guidance of the principles that are generally adopted; such are these who are the object of admiration to their inferiors.—" Such are thy gods, O Israel!"

Though, in the middle ranks of life, there is no great difference of principle, yet we find greater rectitude of conduct, because they are more under the controul, and more under the eye of each other, while the great are exempted from all controul, by the weight and authority they acquire from their wealth: religion, too, has an effect on them, which is seldom felt by their superiors, who have little need of its consolations, and little dread of its terrors: but to found, solid, virtuous principles, resulting from an enlarged view of things, from just notions of happiness, and a benevolent regard to the welfare of others, both of them are equally strangers; and they must ever remain so, till education is conducted by different rules from what it is at present; till it is directed more to correct the heart and morals, than to teach a few points of useless learning; till it is directed more to purposes of social, as well as civil life,

life, to make good men, rather than good soldiers, sailors, and divines. The great object of education at present, is to enable young men to get forward in the world: and into that world they are often turned loose at the age of ten or fifteen years, without any other qualification than a little school learning, and they are thus left to receive the education of chance, not of principles. They are never taught the grand radical principle of social happiness, to do good to others for the sake of their own comfort, but are rather, from all that they see, taught to believe that they have nobody to consider but themselves; if they fall into what is called good hands, and acquire a tolerable regard for reputation, and are preserved from enormous vices, they may arrive at the very highest stations with great success and character, and be held up as models of virtue, though they should be content to see thousands starving around them, while they are revelling in plenty. Education, conducted in this manner, may succeed in acquiring rank and fortune; but no steady, firm, and virtuous principles, can be thus acquired by chance, any more than we should expect a grain of seed to grow up and

and flourish among thorns and thistles. Men so educated, may get through the world even with splendid reputation, but never can act from a steady, constant, and fervent principle of benevolence, by which alone they can be of any service to their fellow creatures, or contribute to improve the condition of the world; for it is by this test that every man's goodness must be tried. Such a man is a very good sort of a man, but what has he done to make others wiser or happier? But after this it may fairly be asked—What is there in the higher ranks to compensate for all these deficiencies? Nothing but their manners, and these have a polish, an ease, and elegance, which give an interest even to the most trifling conversation, which soften the harsher features of vice, and make even virtue more amiable:—such a polish, it is to be wished, might not exclusively belong to one set of people, nor ever be used to disguise meanness, deceit, treachery, and that in all ranks it might be found as the ornament of virtue, truth, and integrity.

But if this want, or depravity of principle, is to be lamented in private society, how much more in the rulers of the world; hence it is, that history is but the record of the crimes and follies of the great, and that so few pages are sufficient for their virtues. Among all the great characters that have appeared on the theatre of the world, how few have been actuated by the steady principle of doing good to mankind, passion or interest have been the great motive of the greatest men; hence it is that the world has been disturbed and desolated, and that ages have passed without any material improvement in the condition of society. The steady persevering efforts of a few individuals have effected much, but little compared with what might have been done by those who had it most in their power: accident, caprice, and the slow moving series of events, have done more for mankind than all those to whose remembrance history has been idly consecrated: let it no longer then be the doubtful, deceitful, or partial record of splendid atchievements, but the faithful narrator of such events only, as have contributed, and may contribute, to private and general improvement.

Morpeth, June 8th. W. B.

THE questions which were proposed in the outset of this enquiry, have in some degree been answered by the stress that has been laid on the necessity of teaching men to act from right principles. Now, all principles are right or wrong, only as they produce happiness or misery, and can, therefore, only be judged by their effects: it is the same in the science of morality, as in all other sciences; if we set out upon wrong principles, or with no principle at all, the consequence must be error, misconduct, and misery. In the one case, the danger is greater than in the other: because in the one, we have nothing to lead us astray but mistake or ignorance, for no appearance of interest can ever deceive us in the pursuits of chemistry, botany, or agriculture; but in all things connected with the conduct of life, or the dealings of men with each other, we are liable to be deceived by passion and prejudice; the great object of principle is to guide and direct us through the mists and darkness which these occasion, to see our own interest, and that of others, as inseparably connected, notwithstanding the false light in which

which they may be placed by these great deceivers of mankind.

The generality of writers on the subject of morality, merely teach us how to avoid evil, without telling us how to do good; they do not enforce the necessity of any constant, active principle of benevolence, suited to all stations and all times: they merely advise to comply with the law of the land, to be true and just in all our dealings, to take things as we find them, &c. Now, these rules may be very well calculated to keep the world as it is, and to make a part of it happy at the expence of the rest; but this is not enough, for happiness is as much the right of one man as another, without we suppose that the Deity sent some men into the world purposely to be miserable, which does not seem probable from the constitution of nature, for all men are born with equal capacities for happiness, and the world contains the means of it for all its inhabitants; yet notwithstanding this, there seems to be a tendency in mankind to counteract all these bright ideas, or else why so much misery in the world: whether this arises from the institutions of society which may be corrected, or from some inherent perverseness

verseness in the nature of man, which no principles can counteract or destroy, time only can determine; for it is certain, that for many ages no just principles have been laid down for the attainment of general happiness, none which seem adequate to the end proposed. Individuals have at all times sought their own private utility, and even that they have pursued by means ill suited to the purpose. Hence, all those vicious institutions founded in injustice, because they have had in view only the advantage of a few, at the expence of the multitude; and though in many countries the spirit of christianity and philosophy have meliorated the condition of the oppressed, yet they have never gone to the root of the evil. Philosophy has indeed done much, because it has pointed out the radical defects and corruptions of many systems of morality, and many political institutions; it has laid open to all, the rights of all, and exposed the iniquity of exclusive privileges not grounded in general utility: it has done more within the last century for the promotion of human happiness, than had been done for many centuries before;

fore; and when the tumults of war, and the turbulence of ambition have subsided, it will resume its seat in the world, and preside over the councils of princes. Without principles, pow , in the hands of a g eat man, is like a sword in the hands of a robber, he uses it only to effect his own purposes, and regards not who bleeds nor who suffers. More particularly then does it concern the world, that men of illustrious birth and great talents should be early taught the great principle of doing good, of considering, in all their actions, their own happiness as connected with that of others— that they should never intend nor undertake any design, without saying to themselves, will this injure any other man? will it produce happiness or misery? am I promoting my own advantage at the expence and cost of others? This is a broad and extensive principle, and adapted to general use, and he who is determined to act on it, must make a deep search into his conduct and his motives, and take a wide survey of things; such a man will, in all the events of life, be constantly superior to the ill effects of his own passions, and those of other people; he
will

will endeavour to see every object in its true light, and make every allowance for the failings and defects of others, for their weakness, temptations, and ignorance; he will pursue with steadiness and firmness, whatever good purpose he has in view, without being diverted from it by the perverseness or contradiction of others; he will trust more to the steady and constant effects of good intentions, than fear the waywardness of caprice and prejudice; and though from the collisions of human passions, he cannot always expect to do good to some without giving offence to others, he will adhere to his purpose and wait for events to justify the wisdom and purity of his intentions: such a man will be happy as far as happiness depends on inward dispositions, and he will make others happy, as far as his fortune will permit him to relieve their wants, and his principles prevent him from disturbing their tranquillity.——Such are the effects which may be produced in the world by the constant operation of virtuous principles. To know how these are to be implanted in the breasts of youth, requires long and attentive experiment; and the consideration of the subject might lead me beyond the bounds of my original purpose, which was at present merely to enforce the necessity of acting upon solid and virtuous principles.

W. B.

Morpeth, Sept. 3, 1800.

FINIS.

ERRATA.

Page 19.—For APOLLO, read THE GOD.
—— 44.—Line 5. for ARE, read IS.
—— 56.—Line 4. from the bottom, after KINDNESS, put ?
——. 110.—Line 2. put only a comma at NATURE, and a period at US.
—— 125.—Line 3. from the bottom, dele OWN.
—— 126.—Line 4. from the bottom, for R. read H.
—— 134.—Sonnet, line 13. for MIRTH read CLAIMS.

Newcastle upon Tyne:—Printed by Matthew Brown.

www.ingramcontent.com/pod-product-compliance
Lightning Source LLC
LaVergne TN
LVHW061214060426
835507LV00016B/1927